Managing Migraines

Dealing with migraines from
all perspectives ... something
to help each sufferer

Claire Houlding

Bloomington, IN Milton Keynes, UK

authorHOUSE®

AuthorHouse™
1663 Liberty Drive, Suite 200
Bloomington, IN 47403
www.authorhouse.com
Phone: 1-800-839-8640

AuthorHouse™ UK Ltd.
500 Avebury Boulevard
Central Milton Keynes, MK9 2BE
www.authorhouse.co.uk
Phone: 08001974150

First published by AuthorHouse 4/24/2007

ISBN: 978-1-4259-7488-6 (sc)

Library of Congress Control Number: 2007901272

Printed in the United States of America
Bloomington, Indiana

This book is printed on acid-free paper.

Managing Migraines

Contents

Foreword

By
Dr. Elliot Shevel
B.D.S., Dip. M.F.O.S., M.B., B.Ch.

Migraines are one of the most common ailments of mankind, affecting young and old alike. Approximately 18 percent of women and 6 percent of men worldwide suffer from migraines, most of whom remain undiagnosed and untreated. Most often, sufferers self-medicate by using harmful, over-the-counter medications.

Many people do however seek medical treatment, especially when the pain is severe, when the attacks are frequent, and when their quality of life is adversely affected. They are often concerned that they may be suffering from a serious neurological condition such as a brain tumor, and seek reassurance. Fortunately, only a small percentage of patients who present with headache have serious or life threatening conditions. Most have migraine or related headache types.

It is common for migraine sufferers to drift from doctor to doctor, to physical therapist, to chiropractor, and to alternative therapist, in an effort to find relief. Eventually many lose hope, become alienated from the medical profession, and often never improve. In too many cases, their condition worsens as a result of the various drugs they are taking in a futile effort to ward off the endless suffering. Their quality of life, interpersonal relationships at home and at work, and their general ability to function on a normal level are compromised. Often this is compounded by a lack of sympathy from those around them.

But many of these unfortunates can be helped. Migraines have been shown to be genetically linked, but this does not mean that they cannot be treated. The problem is that there are so many factors that have an influence on migraines that it can be extremely difficult to pinpoint what is important in each sufferer. Everyone is different, and must be individually assessed. There is no silver bullet!

There are a vast number of books on migraines, but most are written from one perspective only. They are usually written by a therapist who is convinced that their particular philosophy or treatment is the answer to migraines.

In this book on migraine, Claire Houlding shares her own personal experience and her extensive knowledge on the subject. As someone who suffered from migraines for many years, she is well acquainted with the frustrations encountered by migraineurs. Claire has studied the subject from many different perspectives, and as a result has been able to produce this remarkable book. The extensive and detailed information on drug interactions should be compulsory reading for medical practitioners. She has covered the many facets of migraines so comprehensively, that there will, I believe, be few migraine sufferers who do not derive benefit from reading it. Claire's book will allow many, many people to take control and manage their migraines far more efficiently. There is something for everyone in this book.

Dr Elliot Shevel
B.D.S., Dip. M.F.O.S., M.B., B.Ch.
President, South African Headache Society
Medical Director, The Headache Clinic,
Johannesburg, South Africa.

Introduction

In daily practice, I frequently come across migraine sufferers who have reached a state of absolute desperation. They are inadequately informed about their condition, as to the reasons why they get such terrible pains, where the pain originates from, what makes it worse, and how to effectively treat it. Migraines are a complex condition to treat, and often it takes much trial and error to find a treatment. I have spent many hours counseling these patients, and have tried to explain their condition to them and the fact that an effective treatment is not always easy to find. No one particular treatment will be suitable for every sufferer, and therefore it takes time to find the appropriate one for each individual person.

People generally lack complete advice. Every practitioner they approach will usually prescribe his or her remedy in isolation, i.e. a doctor usually gives medicine, a homeopath will give solutions and pilules, an herbalist will give suitable herbs, and a dietician will provide sample diets to follow. However, patients very rarely obtain holistic advice from any particular source. Very often it is actually a combination of numerous different trades that will work very well together to cure a person's problem. For example, painkillers taken in conjunction with some lifestyle modifications, with certain dietary changes, the right vitamins, and perhaps a regular reflexology massage or yoga may well be the holistic solution that a sufferer needs to conquer his pain. I have seen so many migraine sufferers who feel lost and desperate and who have no idea whom to turn to next. I have seen them lose their sense of hopelessness once they find out how many alternatives are actually available to them, and I hope that through this book I can reach many more sufferers and likewise give them an optimistic outlook when they feel despondent and burdened by pain.

I have attempted, in this book, to take a complete look at migraines, and try to address all the common questions I have come into contact with. I have started by explaining where migraines come from, how to diagnose them, which trigger factors can make them worse, and finally have taken an in-depth, objective, and holistic view into their various treatments, from preventative measures to acute treatments. These are dealt with from medicines to vitamins to herbal supplements, and extending to alternative methods such as massage, acupuncture, and yoga, to name only a few examples. In addition, I have included lifestyle modifications, which are known to help with migraines, and have given an example of a migraine diary, which can be used to keep track of your pain and the treatments you've tried.

Again, I cannot overemphasize the fact that it often takes time and patience to find a solution. Do not give up unless you have truly given a remedy a chance to work before moving on to another one. Even then—try, try again, until you find something that suits you. I myself have suffered migraines all of my life, and I know that at times you feel completely downhearted and reach a stage of utter desperation when the pain becomes too much to bear. I hope that this book gives you more insight into your migraines and into the many, many different treatment alternatives that are available to you. If, at any stage, your pain becomes worse or unbearable, then please be sure to contact your doctor immediately for a full check-up to eliminate any other causes for your headaches.

This book is meant to guide you into the many possible alternative treatments that are available to you to cure your migraines, but should not be used in place of medical advice. This book is meant to lend hope to those who feel that everything they have tried has failed, and who think that there is nothing else left for them to try. Please don't despair—there is something out there to suit everyone. All you have to do is find what suits you.

I wish you all the best in finding a solution to your migraines. Hopefully you will find a remedy far sooner than you ever thought possible.

Claire Houlding
B.Pharm (Rhodes) cum laude

Managing Migraines

"The merest schoolgirl when she falls in love,
has Shakespeare or Keats to speak her mind,
but let a sufferer try to describe a pain in his head to a doctor,
and language at once runs dry."

Virginia Woolf

CHAPTER 1

What is a Migraine?

The word "migraine" is derived from the very accurately descriptive Greek word *"hemikrania,"* which means "half the skull." A migraine is a throbbing headache that occurs periodically in some people, usually on one side of the head. Migraines differ from regular headaches in that they are far more intense and have numerous symptoms which are absent in a regular headache. A migraine sufferer may experience certain phases which define a migraine and differentiate it from other headache types, such as the prodromal syndrome, an aura (in classical migraines), the actual migraine headache, and finally, the postdrome.

The cause of a migraine headache is not completely understood, but there are numerous theories. The most common theories are the Vascular Theory, which believes that spasming blood vessels are involved; the Nerve Theory, which maintains that overly active nerve impulses in the brain are the cause; the Neurotransmitter Theory, which states that migraines are caused by an imbalance of certain brain chemicals, such as serotonin; and the Muscular Theory, which claims that migraines are brought about by muscle tension in the jaw, head, neck, and shoulders. All these theories have a place in the cause of a migraine headache, and it is probably a combination of all these theories that is involved in a migraine attack.

Serotonin is a chemical in the brain which has numerous functions. It influences moods, appetite, sleep, pain, and the activity of blood cells and blood vessels. Imbalanced serotonin levels in the brain are thought to bring about the migraine headache, because of the effect of serotonin on the blood vessels. The cause of the serotonin imbalance is unknown, but is believed to be of a genetic nature. It is also believed that a major set of nerves in the head, called the trigeminal nerves, are involved. When this nerve tract is activated, it sends out pain signals via numerous chemicals, which are released. The blood vessels inside and outside the brain become swollen and inflamed, thereby producing more pain.

The migraine starts off when the blood vessels suddenly constrict (narrow), making the patient feel lightheaded. Some people experience visual disturbances—such as flashing spots or zigzagging lines—at this stage, which is termed the aura. Immediately afterward, the vessels dilate (relax and open), and the patient may feel faint or dizzy for a few seconds until blood rushes back into the brain. This is associated with the onset of a throbbing, pulsating headache. Some sources attribute the starting point of a migraine to the clotting of blood platelets, which prevents blood from flowing freely through the blood vessels. This clotting process is thought to be initiated by the serotonin imbalance.

The pulse will seem greatly exaggerated in the relaxed and inflamed vessels in the brain, as these are not resisting the pressure of blood from the heart as they would normally be. This gives rise to the throbbing headache. The pain may extend over the whole head or may be one-sided, as the Greek word *"hemikrania"* implies. The pain may not always occur on the same side of the head. Usually the sufferer will experience pain over an eye or a temple, but it will not always be the same eye or temple. Pain may radiate down the neck to the shoulders. This may be exacerbated, because the patient will be tense, trying not to move their head too much, as this seems to worsen the pain.

The symptoms of flashing lights and zigzagging lines only occur in those who suffer from a classical migraine and are a part of the aura. People who suffer from a common migraine do not experience this aura. The classical migraine occurs less frequently than the common migraine, with only one in five migraine patients experiencing this phenomenon.

About 35 percent of sufferers will know that they are going to have a migraine attack, because they get a selection of signs and symptoms from a few hours to a few days ahead of the migraine, warning them of its onset. This combination of signs and symptoms is called a prodromal syndrome, which includes mood changes, diarrhea or constipation, tiredness, food cravings, and alternating hot and cold sensations, among others.

In some people, a migraine is also associated with tingling or a partial loss of sensation in the body. Sometimes the patient will lose some feeling on one side of the body in the arms, fingers, and even extending down the legs. Sometimes the migraine sufferer experiences drooling, speech problems, confusion, and blackouts.

A migraine does not only affect the head, it also causes symptoms right throughout the body, and very frequently a migraine sufferer will feel strange for many hours or even days after the migraine has subsided. This is termed the postdrome. A sufferer may feel tired, lethargic, moody, disoriented, and may have a dry mouth. Side effects of medicines can also contribute to feelings of tiredness and disorientation.

CHAPTER 2

Who Is Likely to Suffer from Migraines?

It is not yet completely clear why some people will suffer from migraines while others do not. There are numerous theories that suggest that migraines are hereditary. This means that a parent who suffers from migraines may have a child who will likewise be a sufferer.

It is thought that migraine sufferers have an overactive "migraine center" in the brain. This means that when a sensitive person is exposed to numerous stimuli, the nerves in this center of the brain become over-excited and cause a migraine. These stimuli can include foods and drinks, stress, or environmental factors, such as pollution or weather extremes, among other trigger factors. It is unclear why some people are more sensitive than others, and why they will get a migraine when exposed to certain stimuli.

Women are two to three times more likely to suffer from migraines than men, which leads to the belief that female hormones may be involved. Between 60 and 70 percent of women find that during a pregnancy, migraines will improve remarkably, whereas others find that they get worse. This change in migraines could be attributed to the increase in hormones (especially progesterone) coursing through the woman's body in order to sustain the pregnancy.

Migraines may occur in children as young as two years old. As the child reaches puberty, the migraines sometimes stop completely. Generally migraines improve with age, peaking between thirty-five and forty years of age, and then reducing in severity and frequency.

CHAPTER 3

What Could it Be Mistaken As?

A *common headache* is often incorrectly referred to as a migraine. However, there is seldom evidence of any of the other signs and symptoms associated with true migraines, such as nausea, vomiting, light and noise sensitivity, or tingling. Neither will there be an association between common trigger factors and the headache. Treatment of such a headache is generally simple, and rarely requires the more intense therapy needed for treating migraines.

A *tension headache* is sometimes mistaken as a migraine, but in this case, the pain forms a viselike band around the head, which seems to crush the skull. The pain often lasts for days, or even weeks. At times there may be nausea due to the pain, but there will be no prodromal syndrome, aura, or light or noise sensitivity. These headaches are treated with muscle relaxants and anti-inflammatory drugs. Tension headaches can occur together with a migraine, and may even give rise to a migraine attack. Very frequently, migraine sufferers find that when they suffer from a migraine, they feel muscle tension around the head, neck, and shoulders.

Cluster headaches are severely debilitating headaches, occurring at approximately the same time every day for days or weeks. The pain is intense, and is often described as a sensation like having a hot poker stabbing into the eye. Sometimes the eyes and nose will be red and watering, respectively. Cluster headaches are also termed "suicide headaches" because of their intensity. The pain is more a stabbing pain, rather than a pulsating or throbbing one, as in migraines. Again, the prodromal syndrome and aura will be absent. Some theories do exist, however, which state that cluster headaches are a type of migraine.

Chronic sinusitis, which is an infection in the bony cavities (holes) surrounding eyes, in the cheeks, and in the forehead, is caused by bacteria. The cavities become inflamed and swollen, and are often filled with a thick mucus. This causes an increase in pressure in the sinuses, because the bony cavities cannot expand any further, and a pain develops around the eyes, in the forehead, and along the cheekbones. Because of the pain around the eyes and sinuses, this headache is often mistaken for a migraine. This type of headache lasts longer than a usual migraine, and is often associated with a fever and swollen glands. By leaning forward sharply, pain increases dramatically and gives rise to a sensation that the brain is falling to the front of the face. If this is the case, you should consult a doctor and have your sinuses examined. The doctor may prescribe a course of antibiotics to kill the bacteria and decongestant, mucolytic (dissolving mucus) medicines to help clear the mucus out of the sinuses, thereby reducing the pressure. In severe cases, you may need a sinus drainage operation.

Eyestrain, from working in badly lit conditions, always staring at a computer, or needing reading glasses but not being aware of it can be the cause of pain around the eyes. Often nausea will result, and this may give the impression of having a migraine. Having your eyes checked regularly can eliminate some degree of eyestrain, especially if prescription glasses are considered necessary.

Meningitis produces a severe headache, which can be associated with nausea, but there is no prodromal syndrome, and the headache continues on for many days. An important symptom experienced with meningitis is a stiff neck, to the extent that the sufferer finds it impossible to bend their head forward towards their chest. The pain produced in trying to do this is as though the spinal cord is being pulled out. In addition, there will probably be a fever, as the cause of meningitis is bacterial or viral. Antibiotics will be required to treat this headache, together with strong painkillers.

Brain tumors are more complex, but the pain produced here is constant and will not cease. Other symptoms to look out for are lack of movement or control of certain parts of the body, depending on where the tumor is situated. Treatment is very complex in this instance. This is not the most common cause of headaches, and brain tumors are rarely suspected in headache sufferers. CT scans of the head and brain can be performed to establish the presence of a tumor.

It is important to note that different headaches may sometimes overlap. A patient may be suffering from a migraine at the same time he or she is having a tension headache, sinusitis, or any other type of headache. This can complicate the diagnosis of a particular headache.

CHAPTER 4

What Causes a Migraine?

A migraine is caused by the sudden constriction, followed by dilation, of the blood vessels in the head. It is still unclear as to what makes some people more susceptible to suffering from migraines than others. As mentioned, the blood vessels, nerves, and chemicals in the brain all seem to play a role in migraine production.

There are many trigger factors which can bring on a migraine in susceptible people, and about 80 percent of sufferers can identify which ones cause their migraines. Trigger factors cause the sudden reaction in the blood vessels, which gives rise to the migraine. Different trigger factors affect different people, and once you identify which ones affect you, you can learn to avoid them. Trigger factors can be of various different origins, e.g. dietary, physiological, or psychological. These factors do not seem to have any effect in people who do not suffer from migraines.

It may be very useful to keep a headache diary in which you can note down which trigger factor you were exposed to which potentially caused the migraine you are having. You may eventually see a pattern developing, which can help you, as well as your doctor, in identifying harmful factors and to treat you accordingly.

Common Migraine Trigger Factors
Dietary factors
Missed or delayed meals
Stress, disturbed sleeping patterns and anxiety
Weather
Female hormones
Loud noises
Bright, flashing lights
Smoking
Pollution and strong odors
Physical or mental exertion
Medicines

Table showing common migraine trigger factors.

Dietary Factors

There are several foods and beverages which are known to cause migraines in many sufferers. Each dietary factor will not necessarily affect every sufferer. Many people can identify which items give them a migraine. Some of these items contain an amine substance called tyramine, which triggers migraines. This may have to do with the fact that tyramine is metabolized by the same enzyme that inactivates other vital monoamine substances in the body, such as serotonin, adrenaline, and dopamine. An imbalance in these substances, especially in sensitized migraine sufferers, could therefore cause a migraine. Foods and drinks that have been aged, e.g. certain cheeses and red wine, are more likely to set off an attack than their younger alternatives.

Common Dietary Trigger Factors
Alcohol, especially red wine
Artificial sweeteners, e.g. Aspartame
Caffeine in tea, coffee, fizzy drinks and supplements
Cheese, especially aged and strong cheeses, e.g. cheddar, parmesan
Chocolate, especially dark chocolate (higher cocoa content)
Citrus fruits
Ice cream
Meat extracts
Monosodium glutamate (MSG), a flavor enhancer used in Chinese food
Nitrate preservatives
Pickled or fermented foods
Smoked meats, e.g. bacon
Tinned meats
Tomatoes
Wheat
Yeast products

Table showing common dietary trigger factors.

One method of identifying if any of these foods trigger your migraine is to remove them from your diet completely and slowly re-introduce them one by one. If you get a migraine after re-introducing an item, then you know that you will have to avoid it in the future. If no migraine results after re-introducing an item into your diet, then you know that you can safely continue eating or drinking it.

Often quantity is an issue, but not always. Consuming more than one trigger factor at a time, and in large volumes, can bring on a migraine with relative certainty, whereas if you are exposed to only one trigger factor in a smaller magnitude, you may get away without suffering a migraine. Unfortunately, some sufferers are so sensitive that they can feel a migraine start as they eat a single block of dark chocolate. It is very much an individual issue, and each patient must determine his or her own threshold and sensitivity to his or her own trigger factors.

Missed or delayed meals

Missing meals, fad diets, or delayed meals have the potential to cause a migraine. This may be as a result of having too little available blood sugar, or because of the lack of certain foods or food groups in fad diets. A healthy way of maintaining a constant blood sugar level, and hence preventing a migraine, would be to have five smaller meals a day rather than one or two large ones. In addition, in the case of dieting, a lower-calorie diet should be considered, where healthier foods are eaten in smaller quantities, rather than cutting out important food groups, as is the case in many fad weight loss schemes.

Stress, disturbed sleeping patterns and anxiety

Stress definitely plays a role in either bringing on a migraine attack or making an existing one worse. Sufferers often find that they have more migraines when they are stressed. It is also seen repeatedly that some people will have a migraine attack after they have gone through an intensely stressful period, which is termed a "post-stress letdown." As soon as their stress factors are resolved and they are able to relax, a migraine attack occurs.

Stress also increases the amount of adrenaline in the body, which can make sufferers feel tense and even nervous or anxious. In a susceptible person, this can cause a migraine attack.

Insomnia (sleeplessness) is a frequent sign in stressful living. A lack of sleep can cause tiredness, as well as irritability, anxiety, and hence, migraines. Too little or too much sleep can be a trigger to a migraine attack. Sleeping in late on weekends or holidays may be almost as dangerous as getting too little sleep over a busy, stressful week.

Weather

Heat causes vasodilation to help the body cool off. This also occurs in the blood vessels in the head, thus causing a migraine. Stuffy, thick, hot air can be an important trigger to avoid.

Cold weather may cause tension in the body as the body tries to limit movement in order to keep itself warm. The face and head are often exposed, and this may trigger a migraine in susceptible persons.

Similarly, a change in atmospheric pressure may precipitate a migraine attack. Traveling to different climates can often set off a migraine, especially if the climates differ considerably.

Female hormones, i.e. estrogen and progesterone

The effects of these hormones may be exhibited from puberty, when their levels rise. They fluctuate throughout the month and may precipitate a migraine around the time of ovulation, before, during or even after menstruation, depending on the individual woman.

Immediately before ovulation occurs at day 14 of the menstrual cycle, estrogen levels peak and then drop. This can cause a migraine in susceptible women. After ovulation, levels of both these hormones rise again, but progesterone levels peak. Both of these hormones drop off in concentration a couple of days before menstruation begins and this may once again cause a migraine. Most women find that their migraines will be worst around the time of their menstruation, but some suffer mid-cycle, at ovulation. In order to determine the effect of these hormones on a woman's migraines, it might be an idea to monitor the menstrual cycle for a few months to see whether it is ovulation or menstruation that cause the most distress. This will help a doctor to decide on what type of treatment , if any, may be best to prevent the painful effects of these hormone fluctuations. Some doctors may prescribe specific hormone regimens that will be less likely to cause migraines in certain cases.

Similarly in pregnancy, when progesterone levels are high to maintain a healthy placenta for the growing fetus, some women will experience a change in migraine frequency; 60 to 70 percent of women find that their migraines improve during their pregnancy, and that they experience a long term of relief, even after their child has been born. Only a few women experience their first migraine during pregnancy. At menopause, some women may find an increased relief from migraines, when their hormone levels drop.

Loud noises

Most migraine sufferers find that very loud noises that are ongoing or very high-pitched may bring on an attack.

Bright, flashing lights

A susceptible person may not only get a migraine attack when in a disco or cinema, but also from other sources of light, such as from driving in an avenue of trees which intermittently lets through sunlight. The effect of rapidly moving through alternating shade and sun can bring on a migraine. Fluorescent and bright lights can bring on an attack just as easily as flashing lights or even bright, natural daylight.

Smoking

Smoking can cause migraines, because of the nicotine contained in the cigarettes. Nicotine can act on blood vessels, causing them to narrow. Secondary smokers, i.e. people who are exposed to the cigarette smoke of smokers, often suffer migraines as a result of these smokers.

Pollution and strong odors

Polluted air contains many different chemicals, some of which trigger migraines. It may be the strong odor of pollutants such as petrol or gasoline fumes, paint, detergents, and other gases that can cause a migraine. Some sufferers find that even some pleasant-smelling products, such as perfumes, incense, air-fresheners or potent floral smells can trigger their migraines.

Physical or mental exertion

Pushing the body beyond its limits, either physically or mentally, can cause stress levels to increase, thereby putting the sufferer at risk of having a migraine. When the body is physically taxed, especially when the weather is hot and dehydration occurs due to loss of sweat, then a migraine attack is almost inevitable in susceptible people. Whether the stress is physical or mental, adrenaline levels increase in the body in order to help it cope, but this level of stimulation cannot be maintained without something else giving way— in this case, the susceptible individual puts him- or herself at risk of developing a migraine headache.

Medicines

Numerous medicines can trigger a migraine in sufferers. A few of the more common medicines that can cause a migraine are discussed below, but they are by no means the only ones.

Nitroglycerines

These are substances used by angina patients. Angina pectoris is a condition of the heart where the blood vessels surrounding the heart go into a spasm, thereby preventing oxygenated blood from getting to the heart muscle. This produces a sharp chest pain. In order to treat this condition, medicines are given to open up the blood vessels surrounding the heart. A very common side effect of these medicines, i.e. nitroglycerines, is that they also open up the blood vessels in the head, which not only causes flushing, but also a migraine attack to occur. As soon as blood vessels are too dilated, a migraine headache may start.

Hormone pills e.g. oral contraceptives

Oral contraceptive tablets prevent pregnancy by inhibiting ovulation (the release of the egg from the ovaries). In order to do this, the woman is given a daily dose of hormones. To mimic the normal menstrual cycle, there are placebo (inactive) tablets in a pack of contraceptives, during which time the woman will get a monthly bleed. The placebo tablets contain no hormones, and this sudden removal of hormone intake or the renewed hormonal input into the body after the placebo period may bring on a migraine headache. If your migraines continue throughout the month, when you are taking the active hormone tablets, or if your migraines get worse, then you must tell your doctor. Likewise, if you want to start taking an oral contraceptive, you must inform your doctor that you suffer from migraine headaches.

Some women find that their migraines improve while they are taking an oral contraceptive. These are usually women who have defined migraine trigger factors such as certain foods e.g. chocolate, cheese, or red wine. Women who treat their migraine headaches with ergotamines (see chapter on "Treatments for Migraines") should not take the oral contraceptive pill. This is because of the potential for blood clots to be formed in narrowed blood vessels, thereby causing obstruction of blood flow, which could result in a thrombosis in the brain or heart.

Stimulants

Medicines or chemicals which have a stimulating action, such as caffeine (e.g. in tea or coffee, or in stimulant tablets used to prevent drowsiness), ephedrine, or pseudoephedrine (e.g. in slimming pills or cold and flu preparations) can cause excitation, overstimulation, and anxiety. These medicines all have the potential to cause migraines. They increase the heart rate and blood pressure, which increases blood flow to the brain and can cause a pounding headache. If you are a migraine sufferer, then it is better to avoid using stimulants such as these. It is therefore probably contradictory to mention that numerous painkillers and migraine preparations contain a small amount of caffeine. The reason for this addition seems to be firstly to counteract some of the drowsiness caused by these preparations, and secondly to enhance the absorption of the medicines, because gastrointestinal motion is reduced during migraines. If you find that you are very sensitive to caffeine, then rather choose a product which does not contain it. Its content in these tablets, however, will not generally be at a high enough dosage to cause a migraine.

CHAPTER 5

Signs and Symptoms of a Migraine

There are numerous signs and symptoms that occur only in a migraine, which thereby distinguish it from other headaches. Not all these signs and symptoms will necessarily be present with every migraine attack. However, in order for a migraine to be diagnosed, many of these symptoms do need to occur before and during an attack.

Signs and Symptoms associated with Migraine Headaches
Intense throbbing headache
Prodromal syndrome
Aura (visual disturbances, such as flashing lights)
Sensitivity to light
Sensitivity to noise
Sensitivity to strong smells
Nausea and vomiting
Pallor
Muscle weakness
Loss of appetite
Tiredness
Hot and cold spells, including shivering and sweating
Tingling in the hands and feet
Dizziness and confusion
In severe cases even fainting and partial paralysis
Mood changes, irritability and depression

Table showing common signs and symptoms of migraines.

The intense *throbbing, pulsating headache* may be only on one side of the head, and is often localized around one eye or at a temple. The pain may not always be on the same side of the head. The pain often begins early in the morning and can last from four hours to about three days. Some migraine sufferers will experience the pain radiating over the entire head.

About 35 percent of sufferers experience a *prodromal syndrome.* This syndrome occurs from a few hours to a few days before the onset of the migraine and may include mood changes, sweats and chills, nausea, vomiting, frequent urination, constipation or diarrhea, food cravings, stiff neck, and dizziness. These symptoms are seen as a warning that a migraine is about to occur.

There are two major types of migraines: the classical migraine, with an *aura*; and the common migraine without it. A migraine sufferer who experiences an aura will do so at the onset of the migraine, by having visual or other sensory disturbances. The visual effects can vary from brightly colored zigzagging lines to flashing lights or even black spots in their vision. Other symptoms belonging to an aura can be speech defects, lack of movement, loss of feeling or strange tingling sensations in the arms or legs, dizziness, ringing in the ears, or even loss of consciousness. A sufferer would probably only experience one or a few of these sensory disturbances and not necessarily all of them. Only 20 percent of migraine sufferers will experience an aura. No other headache will have these sensory effects. If these sensory disturbances accompany a headache, then the headache is definitely a migraine.

Sensitivity to light, called "photophobia," occurs where sufferers cannot even tolerate looking into normal daylight, let alone fluorescent lights. Light seems to pierce into the eyeballs, making the pain seem even worse. This is a very frequent symptom in migraine sufferers, often starting some time before the actual onset of pain.

Sensitivity to noise, called "phonophobia," is another very common symptom during migraine attacks, where sufferers feel unwell in noisy surroundings.

Many patients exhibit sensitivity to strong smells. Odors coming from substances such as detergents, paint, perfumes, exhaust fumes, petrol or gasoline among other strong-smelling substances, may make a migraine worse.

Nausea and vomiting are the most common symptoms of a migraine, frequently starting a while before the actual onset of the migraine headache. A sufferer will often feel nauseated for no particular reason. It can form a part of the prodromal syndrome, and is used as a warning sign by many patients. Nausea frequently progresses until the patient vomits. Vomiting can alleviate the pain. Many sufferers will find that the headache, as well as other symptoms, such as light and noise sensitivity, improves after they have vomited.

Associated with the nausea and vomiting is another common sign of a migraine, *pallor.* The sufferer becomes very pale and looses all facial color.

Muscle weakness and loss of strength often accompany a migraine, where the patient feels as though he or she has to sit or lie down. The patient feels drained of all energy.

Loss of appetite is experienced, probably due to the fact that intestinal motion lessens as the migraine sets in. Loss of appetite could also be as a result of the nausea or vomiting.

Tiredness and lethargy are familiar symptoms to sufferers, often also serving as warning signals that a migraine attack is imminent. These symptoms regularly extend into the postdrome, after the pain has subsided. This leaves the sufferer feeling weak and tired for hours or days afterwards.

Alternating *hot and cold spells,* including shivering and sweating, make the patient feel very uncomfortable.

Tingling in the hands and feet are less-frequent symptoms, which are felt generally by those who get very severe migraines.

Dizziness and confusion make the patient feel disoriented, and can make nausea worse if the patient does not lie down soon after these symptoms begin.

In severe cases, even *fainting* and *partial paralysis* may occur, where the patient can lose some feeling on one side of his or her body, in an arm, in a hand, or even reaching down to a leg.

Mood changes, irritability, and depression frequently occur well before the migraine sets in, and can be used as a warning sign in observant sufferers. Patients often feel upset or moody for no particular reason, even days in advance of a migraine.

CHAPTER 6

Diagnosis of a Migraine

Migraines are one of the most under-diagnosed conditions. Many doctors are hesitant to diagnose a migraine if the prodromal syndrome or the aura are absent. Unfortunately, only a relatively small percentage of sufferers actually experience these symptoms, leaving many migraine patients undiagnosed and inadequately treated. If an aura is present, the migraine can be diagnosed immediately. If not, then other factors need to be taken into account.

Diagnostic guidelines have been set up for doctors in order to identify a migraine and exclude other possible headache causes, such as chronic sinusitis, tumors, and meningitis, among others. Often a patient will need to have a brain scan in order to make sure that the headache is not as a result of a more serious underlying cause.

The frequency and severity of the headaches are important, as well as identifying how the headaches interfere with your quality of life and daily functioning. The patterns of your migraines can be helpful.

The time at which they usually occur, such as in the early morning or afternoon; during stressful times or afterward; or after eating, drinking, or otherwise being exposed to certain trigger factors are all extremely useful hints as to whether your headache is a migraine. If one or more trigger factors can be identified as generally having been involved with the onset of a migraine, then you have come a long way in helping yourself prevent further migraines. Avoid the trigger factors if you can. If you do not know which trigger factors cause your migraines, your doctor or pharmacist can suggest some of the more common ones, which you can exclude completely from your diet or lifestyle if possible, and re-introduce them slowly back into your life (see chapter on "What Causes a Migraine" for a list of common trigger factors). Those which bring on a migraine are your particular migraine trigger factors and should be avoided.

As will be discussed later, the keeping of a headache diary with all this relevant information can facilitate more accurate diagnosis, and hence more effective pain management.

Signs and symptoms can be very useful in identifying a migraine, because many of them do not occur with other types of headaches. Be sure to mention all the symptoms that you suffer from when you get a migraine, to help your doctor in diagnosing you—especially the presence of an aura, a prodromal syndrome, nausea, vomiting, light, noise, and smell sensitivity.

The location of the headache is very important. Migraine sufferers often have pain over one eye or at a temple.

Intensity of pain can aid in diagnosing a migraine, because the pain is a throbbing, pulsating one, as opposed to an ongoing, dull pain or a sharp, piercing pain.

A collection of specific signs and symptoms generally constitutes a migraine, and mentioning as many as you can remember will help the doctor to eliminate other diagnoses.

CHAPTER 7

Treatment of Migraines

When Elvis Presley died and his blood was analyzed, traces of numerous medicines known to be used for the treatment and prevention of migraines were found. These included ergot alkaloids, anti-nauseants, beta-blockers, and other painkillers. Elvis was a known migraine sufferer, and it was thought that he abused LSD, an illicit recreational drug, which is also classified as an ergot alkaloid. An interesting question may result from this, which is whether his death was actually due to overdosing on medicines to treat his debilitating migraine pain or whether he was in fact taking illicit drugs for recreational purposes. The intensity of the pain of a migraine is seldom understood by non-sufferers, but frequently leads sufferers to a point of desperation to clear the excruciating pain. Often, in an attempt to clear the migraine, sufferers do not think rationally, and take any painkillers they can get their hands on, often in excessive quantities, to stop the throbbing, blinding pain.

The treatment of a migraine is diverse, and experienced migraine sufferers will usually know which therapy suits them best. Treatment is divided up into preventative measures, which will avert a migraine attack, and into cures, which will alleviate an acute migraine attack as it happens. There are many supplementary treatments available, which have proven to be very useful in not only preventing migraines, but also in curing them when they occur.

Treatment should be accompanied by bed rest in a dark room where noise has been blocked out. Sleep is extremely important in treating a migraine.

Not every treatment works for every patient, and often a trial period is necessary to establish which therapy best suits each individual patient. It is important to note that you should communicate with your doctor and pharmacist as to how you feel on your therapy. They will be able to guide you with respect to outcomes and side effects, and answer any questions you may have regarding your medication. Be sure to mention if your migraines do not improve, and especially if they get worse. There are so many variations of therapies available that it is possible to find one that suits you. Try not to give up too soon on a particular preventative therapy. It may take weeks or even months to take effect. During this period, you may still take painkillers if necessary, but check with your doctor or pharmacist if there are any interactions.

THERAPIES USED FOR MIGRAINE HEADACHES

1. Medicinal Treatment

   a. Therapeutic Treatments

      Non-steroidal anti-inflammatory drugs (anti inflammatories)

      Analgesics (painkillers)

      Ergot alkaloids

      Anti-emetics (anti-nausea and vomiting)

      Triptans

      Serotonin antagonists

      Combination therapies

      Migraine cocktails

   b. Prophylactic (Preventative) Therapies

      Beta-blockers

      Tricyclic antidepressants

      Calcium channel blockers

      Alpha agonists

      Anti-epileptics

2. Herbal Supplements

      Feverfew

      St. John's wort

      Kava kava

3. Helpful Vitamins and Minerals

    Magnesium

    Vitamin B

    Omega-3 Essential Fatty Acid

    Trimethylglycine

4. Alternative Therapies

    Homeopathy

    Tissue salts

    Aromatherapy

    Reflexology

    Acupuncture & acupressure

    Massage

    Chiropractic

    Yoga

    Posture-modifying appliance

Medicines Used to Treat and Prevent Migraines

A. THERAPEUTIC TREATMENTS FOR MIGRAINES

Therapeutic medicines are used to treat an existing, acute migraine attack. They are most effective if taken as soon as possible after the onset of the migraine headache. If, however, you find that you are having too many migraines, i.e. more than two or three per month, and that they are so severe that these medicines barely help to alleviate the pain, then you should see your doctor, who may prescribe a preventative therapy for you, which will reduce the severity as well as the frequency of your migraines. Care must be taken to observe the dosage instructions in therapeutic medicines, and to not use them too often, because some of them may become less effective with overuse. Some of these medicines may also bring on headaches if used too frequently, called "rebound headaches." This turns into a vicious circle, because then more medicine needs to be taken to alleviate more pain, eventually leaving the sufferer with nothing being effective anymore. Speak to your pharmacist or doctor if you are worried about taking these medicines, especially if you take them very often.

In addition, to treat a migraine most effectively when it occurs, it is best to lie down in a darkened, quiet room after taking the medicine. Sleep is extremely therapeutic, and being isolated from noises, light, smells and other aggravating factors can help to ease the pain faster. Many migraine treatments have the potential to cause drowsiness, and it is therefore advisable not to drive a car or operate heavy machinery.

NON-STEROIDAL ANTI-INFLAMMATORY DRUGS (NSAIDs)

Non-steroidal anti-inflammatory drugs are medicines that, in simple terms, are referred to as "anti-inflammatories." This very large group of medicines is very useful in treating pain, inflammation, and fever. Anti-inflammatories interrupt the pathway in the body which produces and exacerbates inflammation. Thereby they prevent the inflammation from occurring and pain from being felt. They work best the sooner they are taken after the onset of the migraine. The longer a cycle of inflammation is allowed to continue, the worse the outcome of inflammation may be. A migraine can be aborted completely if the anti-inflammatory is taken during the prodromal stage of a migraine, or if a sufferer knows his or her body well enough to feel that he or she will be getting a migraine.

Inflammation is usually exhibited by certain signs, including redness, swelling, fever, pallor (lack of color), and loss of proper movement. In migraines, some of these symptoms cannot be seen, as they are happening in the blood vessels of the head. The blood vessels become swollen and no longer function as they are meant to because they are inflamed. The sufferer may feel alternatingly hot and cold. By taking an anti-inflammatory, the inflammatory cycle is aborted, and the pain should abate.

Many anti-inflammatories can be bought without a prescription, e.g. aspirin and ibuprofen, and for some of them you may only be able to obtain a five-day supply without prescription. It is always better to start with a weaker anti-inflammatory and then build up to a stronger one if necessary.

Anti-inflammatories are a very widely used group of medicines, and are generally fairly safe to take. There are, however, certain patients who must be very careful about taking an anti-inflammatory, because these may interact with their medication or condition. These patients must always speak to their doctor or pharmacist before taking an anti-inflammatory.

Asthmatics must be careful when using anti-inflammatories, especially aspirin, because they can trigger an asthma attack.

Usually it is only aspirin that causes a problem, but caution must nevertheless be exercised when taking another type, e.g. ibuprofen. If an asthmatic has taken aspirin before and has had no reaction, then there will probably be no interaction, but it is still safer to check with your doctor or pharmacist.

Anti-inflammatories, especially if used frequently or long-term, can cause stomach ulcers, so they must always be taken after food. Patients who suffer from stomach ulcers must be extremely careful about taking anti-inflammatories because of their potential to not only cause a stomach ulcer, but also to aggravate an existing one and perhaps cause stomach bleeding. Your doctor may advise you to take the first one or two doses on an empty stomach in order for the medicine to take effect faster, but thereafter, anti-inflammatories must be taken on a full stomach. Sensitive patients may want to consider using a suppository or an injectable anti-inflammatory, e.g. indomethacin or diclofenac suppositories or injections. These dosage forms are less likely to irritate the stomach and can be used instead of a tablet.

Patients who have kidney disease, problems with fluid retention, or a history of kidney stones must speak to their doctor about taking anti-inflammatories, because these medicines are excreted via the kidney and may cause problems.

Patients who have suffered a stroke or heart attack and are taking medication must speak to their doctor if they want to use an anti-inflammatory.

During pregnancy it is not recommended to take anti-inflammatories, because they may affect labor and blood flow to the fetus. Rather, speak to your doctor beforehand.

Other medical problems which may be aggravated by the use of an anti-inflammatory include diabetes, liver disease, epilepsy, anemia and other blood disorders, porphyria, high blood pressure, and Parkinson's disease.

Numerous medicines interact with anti-inflammatories. Your doctor may prescribe an anti-inflammatory for you, which you must take only as directed, and you must see your doctor for regular check-ups. Under a doctor's supervision, it may be safe to take anti-inflammatories with some of these medicines, but do not take them without consulting your doctor first.

Patients who are on warfarin or other medicines which are used to prevent blood clotting must always be careful when taking anti-inflammatories, because these medicines can cause internal bleeding to occur. Some anti-inflammatories will interfere with the actions of medicines that prevent blood clotting, and hence taking them together may be very dangerous.

Low-dose aspirin is often used to prevent blood clotting. A dosage of 80 to 100 mg is considered a low dose. Taking aspirin or another anti-inflammatory in addition to this low dose will effectively raise the dose to a higher level, thereby negating the anti-clotting effect. The body's default reaction then comes into play, thus allowing the blood to form clots. Any patient taking low-dose aspirin should never take additional aspirin in higher doses for other ailments, such as headaches or fevers, because of this phenomenon. These patients must speak to their doctor or pharmacist before taking an anti-inflammatory, because the interaction can be hazardous.

Other therapies which may be affected by anti-inflammatory use include certain cancer chemotherapy, diuretics (water pills), blood pressure reducing agents, lithium, valproic acid, phenytoin, and medicines used to treat heart and blood disorders.

Side effects may occur, but usually with long-term use and high doses. It is not advisable to use more than one anti-inflammatory at a time, because it can increase the risks of producing more unwanted side effects. The more common side effects include dizziness, drowsiness, stomach ulcers, stomach cramps, indigestion, nausea, vomiting, skin rashes, and sun sensitivity, i.e. the ability to get sunburned. Most of these effects are mild and can be avoided. If they get worse or become unbearable, you must see your doctor or pharmacist. A severe type of allergic reaction, called anaphylactic shock, may occur in people who are allergic to anti-inflammatories, especially asthmatics. If this happens, an ambulance must be called immediately.

Never give aspirin to a child younger than fourteen years of age for a migraine, because it can cause Reye's syndrome, which results in organ failure and could cause death. Rather use mefenamic acid or ibuprofen.

If you are using anti-inflammatories without a prescription, always follow the dosage instructions on the package insert, and do not use more medicine than necessary. Check with your pharmacist or doctor if you are not sure how to use the medicine correctly or if you have concerns about it. Try not to use anti-inflammatories on an ongoing basis without having a check-up from your doctor. If, after five days of taking anti-inflammatories, you still suffer from your migraine, you should consult your doctor.

Examples of NSAIDs used to treat migraines:

Aspirin (BayerAspirin®, Disprin®)

Ibuprofen (Advil®, Motrin®)

Diclofenac (Voltaren®, Cataflam®)

Mefenamic acid (Ponstan®)

Indomethacin (Indocid®)

Naproxen (Aleve®)

ANALGESICS (Painkillers)

Analgesics are medicines that stop the pain by interfering with the pain pathway in the body. They are generally very safe to use. The most common painkiller available is acetaminophen, which alleviates mild pain and fever. It is available without a prescription. Acetaminophen is usually the painkiller of choice as a first option in treating pain because of its safety profile.

Acetaminophen works very well for mild to moderate pain, but may not always be sufficient to alleviate a migraine. Do not use more medicine than recommended in your package insert. Rather, speak to your pharmacist or doctor, who can advise you on another remedy.

Acetaminophen can be given to young children, adults, and pregnant women who have headaches, as long as the dosage recommendations are followed. If you have taken it for ten days (or five days if a child) and your migraine has still not improved, then you must see your doctor or pharmacist. Do not use ongoing for longer than this period of time without consulting your health care professional. If used ongoing, acetaminophen can cause liver damage.

Use acetaminophen with caution if you have had severe kidney or liver disease. Do not drink alcohol together with acetaminophen, as it may cause liver damage.

There are very few side effects with acetaminophen and they are seen very rarely in therapeutic doses, but they include skin rash and nausea. If used in overdose or long-term, it may cause liver or kidney problems.

Examples of analgesics used to treat migraines:

Acetaminophen (Tylenol®)

ERGOT ALKALOIDS

Ergot alkaloids are extracted from a fungus, called *Claviceps purpurea*, which grows on rye. This medicine causes the blood vessels in the brain to constrict, thereby easing the pain of the migraine. Ergotamines are extremely effective in some migraine sufferers, up to a point of being the only medication that will cure their pain. Even so, other migraine sufferers find little relief after taking an ergotamine.

Dependence develops quickly if ergot alkaloids are used for more than two to three days a week. Rebound headaches occur on an almost daily basis if ergotamine, which has been used too regularly, is withdrawn, and this pain can only be alleviated by taking more ergotamines. This medication should only be used in severe and infrequent migraine attacks. It is most effective if taken as soon as the migraine announces itself, preferably in the prodromal stage. This aborts the migraine much faster than taking it at a later stage. Lying down in a dark, quiet room after taking medicine will further help to clear the migraine.

Ergotamine treatment is not recommended for use in numerous medical conditions, including any type of heart disease, high blood pressure, hyperactive thyroid, kidney and liver disease, anemia, and porphyria, as well as in pregnancy.

It may interact with certain medicines, which include certain antidepressants (e.g. fluoxetine), beta-blockers (e.g. propranolol), some antibiotics (i.e. macrolides, such as erythromycin, and also tetracyclines), and stimulants (e.g. ephedrine). Smokers are also more at risk of developing unwanted effects when taking ergotamines. Patients are advised not to take triptans within six hours of taking ergotamines. It would be worthwhile to check with your doctor or pharmacist if you are considering taking an ergotamine and are also on other medication, in case there is an interaction.

Side effects are fairly common with ergotamines, even at recommended doses, and include nausea and vomiting, drowsiness, confusion, diarrhea, blood pressure increases, increased or decreased heart rate, and pain in the chest. To prevent nausea and vomiting, it is usually advisable to take an anti-emetic half an hour before ergotamine. Some products have an anti-emetic included in the formulation. Cold and tingling in the hands and feet are other side effects, and if this or heaviness in the chest occurs, then the medication must be stopped immediately. If the recommended dosage has been exceeded, then the chance of side effects is greatly increased, and the sufferer may experience swelling of the face, hands, and feet; serious heart effects; tingling and lack of feeling in the body; blue fingers and toes; dizziness; and even gangrene.

Examples of ergot alkaloids used to treat migraines:

Ergotamine (Cafergot®, Migril®)

ANTI-EMETICS

Anti-emetics are medicines that treat or prevent nausea and vomiting. Migraine sufferers frequently suffer from nausea, even well before the onset of the migraine, in the prodromal phase. This also makes it difficult to swallow painkillers, because everything that is taken by mouth is brought up. In addition, vomiting causes dehydration, i.e. loss of fluids and important minerals and salts that the body needs. Dehydration can make a migraine worse. In addition, the movement of the intestines is reduced during a migraine, which can contribute to the nausea.

If an anti-emetic is taken and vomiting is suppressed for half an hour thereafter, the chances are that a painkiller will also stay down and be able to treat the pain. Try to suppress the vomiting reflex for about half an hour after taking the anti-emetic. It is not easy and also not always possible, but will benefit you if you can manage to do it.

In certain cases, where nausea and vomiting are severe, it may be a better idea to use a suppository, which will prevent these symptoms and enable the sufferer to take other medication. Injections are also available, which can be administered by your doctor or a nurse.

Some of the anti-emetics are available without a prescription, whereas the more potent ones will require a doctor's prescription. Metoclopramide is often used as the anti-emetic of choice, because it not only helps with the nausea and vomiting, but also increases the movement of the intestines, thereby making the absorption of other medicines, e.g. painkillers, possible.

The major side effect of these medicines is drowsiness, which can help the sufferer in sleeping away the migraine, but may be a problem for those who cannot lie down. Caution must be exercised if driving or operating machinery. Prochlorperazine is least likely to cause drowsiness, and may be the medicine of choice in situations where the sufferer cannot stop working. Sometimes the mouth may feel dry and vision can become blurred, but this is rare.

In pregnancy it is safer to use buclizine or phosphorylated sugars.

An anti-emetic which is sometimes used, especially in children and pregnant women is an "invert" or phosphorylated sugar. This comes as a sweet syrupy liquid and is taken every fifteen minutes until nausea subsides. The sweet taste of this syrup often puts patients off taking it, but it has its usefulness in treating nausea when stronger medicines are not advised, such as when there is the potential to interact with other medicines or because of certain medical conditions. Diabetics and renal patients should however avoid the use of this product.

Examples of anti-emetics used to treat nausea and vomiting:

Cyclizine (Marezine®, Valoid®)

Prochlorperazine (Stemetil®)

Metoclopramide (Maxeran®, Maxolon®)

Domperidone (Motilium®)

Buclizine (Vomifene®)

Phosphorylated sugars (Emetrol®)

TRIPTANS

Triptans are the latest development in migraine treatments. They act on certain serotonin receptors in the brain. There are numerous types of serotonin receptors. The ones which are stimulated by the triptans are called $5\text{-}HT_1$ receptors. They tend to prevent the release of harmful chemicals in the brain which cause the sensation of pain, and which also cause inflammation of the blood vessels in the brain. By these actions, a migraine headache is very rapidly aborted, often within half an hour to one hour. They are the fastest-acting pain relievers of migraine headaches, and are used exclusively for migraines. They are not always used as first-line treatment, and are generally prescribed if regular painkillers or anti-inflammatories do not help to alleviate the pain. They should never be used as a preventative measure, only as treatment once the migraine has started. The sooner a triptan is taken after the onset of a migraine, the faster it will work, and the more effective it will be. However, they are still extremely effective, even when taken some time after the onset of the migraine. Triptans should only be given if a migraine has been diagnosed, and not for any other type of headache.

The first dose is generally effective, but a further dose can usually be taken after two to four hours if the migraine has not subsided. This depends on which triptan is being used. Triptans also work best if you are able to lie down in a quiet, dark room after taking them. One of the greatest advantages of taking a triptan is that they do not always produce heavy drowsiness, which allows the sufferer to continue with their day as normal.

Another advantage is that they exist as various dosage forms, i.e. tablets, wafers which dissolve rapidly under the tongue, nasal sprays, and injections. In this way, vomiting sufferers, who cannot manage to keep down a pill, will be able to inject themselves with the triptan or use a nasal spray dosage form.

Triptans should never be overused, because the body can get used to them.

Triptans should be avoided if you have heart disease, uncontrolled high blood pressure, liver or kidney problems, or if you have had a stroke.

This medication can be used in conjunction with other painkillers, except ergotamines. Ergotamines must be avoided within at least six hours of taking a triptan. Beta-blockers used to prevent migraines can cause the level of some triptans to be elevated, so your doctor may advise a lower dosage. If you are taking monoamine oxidase inhibitors (MAOI) for depression, then you cannot take a triptan. Triptans cannot be used within two weeks of taking an MAOI. Inform your doctor if you are taking lithium, because it may also interact.

Side effects are rare and usually disappear within two to three hours of taking this medicine. The most common side effects are tiredness, drowsiness, dizziness, weakness, cramps, flushing, and tingling. Less common side effects, which are more serious, include chest pains and difficulty in breathing.

Triptans are very effective at treating an acute migraine attack and work extremely quickly to bring about relief. However, they should not be used regularly or to prevent a migraine.

Examples of triptans used to treat migraines:

Sumatriptan (Imitrex®, Imigran®)

Rizatriptan (Maxalt®)

Zolmitriptan (Zomig®)

Eletriptan (Relpax®)

Naratriptan (Amerge®, Naramig®)

SEROTONIN ANTAGONISTS

Cyproheptadine is very seldom used in the treatment of migraines. It acts on certain histamine and serotonin receptors in the brain, and thereby alleviates the pain. It is not used frequently, but has been found to be relatively effective in children who suffer from migraines. Its side-effect profile tends to limit its use in adults.

Cyproheptadine can be used to treat a migraine attack as it happens or to prevent migraines from occurring. In treating an attack, one tablet is given and repeated after half an hour if necessary. The first two doses are generally sufficient to treat a migraine, but relief can be maintained with one tablet every six hours.

Patients who have other medical conditions such as glaucoma, peptic ulcer disease, prostatic hypertrophy, or bladder or bowel obstruction must avoid taking cyproheptadine. It is also not recommended during pregnancy.

Some medicines will be affected by cyproheptadine, those being monoamine oxidase inhibitors, sleeping pills, and tranquilizers.

Side effects are relatively common, and they include drowsiness, increased appetite, weight gain, confusion, hallucinations, irritability, impotence, nervousness, and sensitivity to sunburn with ongoing use. It is not recommended to drive a car or operate machinery while on this medication.

Examples of serotonin antagonists available:

Cyproheptadine (Periactin®)

COMBINATION THERAPIES

Although it is always better to take as little medicine as possible in the lowest effective dosage, in some cases, where migraines are so intense, a single treatment on its own is not always effective. There are so many combinations available on the market, many of which are identical, but have different names. Combination medicines usually contain more than one painkiller and/or anti-inflammatory, and may even have a muscle relaxant or anti-emetic included. Taking combinations increases the risk of side effects, and patients should always check on the content to exclude possible allergies or medical interactions. It may be a good idea to ask your pharmacist whether the combination is safe for you, considering your current medicines and medical conditions.

Combinations should only be tried if simple therapies, such as painkillers or anti-inflammatories do not work on their own. Once a sufferer has started on a combination treatment, it becomes very tempting to use it every time, instead of using something milder. It becomes an easy way out of the painful migraine, and unfortunately, some combinations are fairly addictive. Combinations containing the strong painkiller codeine are extremely effective, which increases the likelihood of addiction. The addiction may not just be physical—there is a definite psychological component too, in which sufferers will take tablets just in case they may get a migraine.

Codeine is a strong painkiller that is used for moderate to severe pain. It is only available without a prescription in combination therapies. Its major side effects include constipation, drowsiness, liver and kidney damage, depressed breathing, and of course, addiction. Tolerance develops to codeine, which means that with frequent use, its effectiveness decreases, and higher doses become necessary to treat the same level of pain. This is a very dangerous sign, and if tolerance develops to the codeine-containing preparation, then you must stop using it immediately and speak to your doctor or pharmacist. If you feel that you may be using too much medication to treat frequent migraines, then speak to your doctor about it.

Ongoing use of this type of medication can lead to a vicious circle, and give rise to what are termed "drug rebound headaches." This is when the medication actually causes headaches when it is not taken. The body gets so used to having the ongoing input of these combinations that when they are withdrawn, the lack of medication causes a rebound pain to occur. This is very difficult and also quite unpleasant to treat.

If used with caution, combinations are very effective in treating migraine headaches, but a weaker painkiller or anti-inflammatory should always be tried first, because they carry less of a risk of developing dependence or tolerance.

Examples of combination therapies available:

Acetaminophen and ibuprofen

Acetaminophen, ibuprofen, and codeine

Acetaminophen, doxylamine, codeine, and caffeine

Acetaminophen and codeine

Aspirin and acetaminophen

Aspirin, acetaminophen, and codeine

If you are getting more than two to three bad migraines per month that are so debilitating that they affect your social and professional life, then you should see your doctor so that a suitable migraine prevention program can be implemented for you which is not addictive and can reduce the severity and frequency of your attacks. In addition, the doctor can exclude other potential causes for your headache.

MIGRAINE COCKTAILS

Many pharmacies sell "migraine cocktails." These can include various different components to treat a migraine attack. Generally the combination includes a strong painkiller, e.g. codeine; an anti-inflammatory, e.g. ibuprofen; something for nausea and vomiting, e.g. cyclizine; and often clonidine. Some pharmacies also include an ergot alkaloid, in which case you need to ensure that you can safely take it, depending on your current medical conditions or medicines. When you feel as though you need to buy a migraine cocktail, always ask the pharmacist what they put into it, just to make sure that you are not allergic to any of the ingredients, and also to give you an idea of what side effects you can expect.

Migraine cocktails are quick fixes and should not be used too regularly. It is always a better idea to identify which component of the cocktail helps you most, and to then buy some separately, i.e. if you find that the anti-inflammatory seems to be effective on its own most of the time and you are not experiencing nausea or other symptoms at the time, then purchase a supply of the anti-inflammatory. Rather, reserve this more aggressive type of treatment for worse migraines. If you use migraine cocktails for all attacks, even the mild ones, then you may find that your body becomes accustomed to the cocktail, and taking an anti-inflammatory on its own, even for mild migraines, will not seem to work anymore.

It is always better to use the mildest effective treatment at the lowest possible dosage to reduce unwanted side effects and the risk of dependence.

B. PROPHYLACTIC (PREVENTATIVE) THERAPIES

Preventative medicines are taken over an extended period of time—usually six months or longer—to reduce migraine frequency and severity. If taken correctly, these medicines have proven to be extremely useful in improving the quality of life of the migraine sufferer. Many patients experience long-term relief, even after they have stopped taking these medicines. It is important to note that none of these medicines should be stopped abruptly if therapy has continued over a period of several months. Doses should rather be reduced over some weeks. Tapering off of doses should be done under the doctor's direct supervision and with his approval.

BETA-BLOCKERS

This type of medicine works by blocking certain sites in the body, called beta-receptors, which influence the activity of the blood vessels. Beta-blockers thereby prevent the blood vessels in the brain from suddenly constricting (tightening) and then dilating (relaxing), which is what causes the migraine. Beta-blockers are usually taken three times daily and over several months in order for them to exert their full effect. After taking them daily for a few weeks, the body starts to generate more beta-receptors, which are the sites blocked by the medicine. Because of this, it is absolutely essential that you do not suddenly stop taking your medicine. If you do, you are at risk of causing an overstimulation of these sites, which could lead to severe heart palpitations (very rapid heartbeat). In order to prevent this type of reaction, your dosage will be gradually reduced until you can safely stop taking your medicine. This is done through your doctor, who will advise you to take less than your standard dose for one to two weeks, and then reduce it further for a few weeks until you can discontinue your therapy completely.

The results of taking this medicine for migraines have been very positive, and many migraine sufferers have been prescribed beta-blockers.

Asthmatics should not be treated with beta-blockers, because this medicine may cause breathing problems. In diabetics, this medication may increase the risk of hyperglycemia (high blood sugar), and may also mask the warning signs of hypoglycemia (low blood sugar). Be sure to mention to your doctor if you have any other medical conditions to ensure that there will be no dangerous interactions, e.g. emphysema, heart disease, kidney or liver disease, mental depression, overactive thyroid, or myasthenia gravis.

The most common side effects include a very slow heartbeat, tiredness or fatigue, cold hands and feet, decreased libido, and dizziness or light-headedness, as well as mild depression. Many of these will disappear as your body adjusts to the medicine. If, however, these side effects continue or bother you, then check with your doctor or pharmacist, who can advise you on what to do. Rather than discontinuing your therapy because of undesired side effects, speak to your doctor or pharmacist.

Beta-blockers remain as one of the most popular and most successful of migraine prevention therapies. They are only available with a doctor's prescription.

Examples of beta-blockers used to prevent migraines:

Propranolol (Inderal®)

Atenolol (Tenormin®)

TRICYCLIC ANTIDEPRESSANTS

Tricyclic antidepressants are classified as antidepressants, but also have many other uses, one of them being pain control in migraines. They are only available on prescription.

Their exact mode of action is not completely understood, but they are thought to increase the levels of serotonin in the brain as one of their actions. Tricyclic antidepressants work on the nerves in the brain and increase the amount of serotonin available between the nerve cells. Serotonin is an important chemical and has wide uses throughout the body. One method of increasing the concentration of this substance is to take a tricyclic antidepressant. As mentioned before, migraines seem to be brought on in people who have a serotonin imbalance, and hence tricyclic antidepressants have been widely prescribed to migraine sufferers, with a very good rate of success.

Another theory is that people who suffer from ongoing or frequent pain, which can be debilitating, often feel helpless and get frustrated and depressed, and therefore the use of tricyclic antidepressants is well accepted.

Tricyclic antidepressants usually take two to three weeks to show effect, but this may extend as long as six weeks. They are generally administered as a once-daily dose, best taken at night after food and before bedtime. You may be started on a low dose, and if necessary, this dose may be increased. Generally, a low dose will be sufficient to control migraine headaches. You will generally need to take this medicine daily for six months in order to obtain maximum benefit and pain relief.

Tricyclic antidepressants should be used with caution in certain medical conditions, such as glaucoma; asthma; heart, prostate, kidney, or liver disease; overactive thyroid; blood and seizure disorders; and if you have difficulty in passing urine. Make sure that your doctor knows about any other medical conditions that you may have. In some instances, and under your doctor's close supervision, you may still be prescribed tricyclic antidepressants even if you have such conditions, but ensure that you take your medication exactly as prescribed.

If you are taking a monoamine oxidase inhibitor (MAOI), e.g. tranylcypromine, for depression, you must tell your doctor, because there may be a potentially serious interaction with tricyclic antidepressants. Other medicines to be aware of are Cimetidine for ulcers; appetite suppressants, e.g. norpseudoephedrine; medicines for a blocked nose, hay fever, colds, and sinus problems, e.g. pseudoephedrine; and sleeping pills, e.g. diazepam. Other than these considerations, it is fairly safe to take tricyclic antidepressants.

Although tricyclic antidepressants are very widely used, they can have certain side effects, such as drowsiness, dry mouth, constipation, increased appetite (especially a craving for sweets), and weakness.

Most of these will improve after a few weeks, once your body has become used to taking the medication.

Less common side effects include blurred vision, problems with passing urine, irregular heartbeat, stiffness or strange movements in your arms and legs, reduced libido, sore throat, and fever. If these particular side effects occur, you should contact your doctor.

> Examples of tricyclic antidepressants used to prevent migraines:
>
> Amitriptyline (Elavil®)
>
> Imipramine (Tofranil®)

CALCIUM CHANNEL BLOCKERS

Calcium channel blockers are used less frequently than beta-blockers and tricyclic antidepressants, but have shown to be very effective in treating migraines, especially for classical migraines.

Their mode of action is fairly complicated and involves the blood vessels. In migraines, blood vessels suddenly narrow and then widen again. In order for blood vessels to narrow and widen, numerous mechanisms are involved, one of which includes the movement of calcium into the cells. Calcium channel blockers prevent this action, and thereby prevent the blood vessels from suddenly reacting as they do in migraines. This medication stops the unexpected tightening of the blood vessels, and also the widening which follows directly thereafter.

Calcium channel blockers are generally taken as a once-daily dose at bedtime. Therapy may be necessary for several months before it is fully effective. Once treatment has ended, relief from migraines is generally successful for a long time.

Flunarazine has few interactions with other medicines or conditions, which makes it much more popular than verapamil, which should be used with caution in patients with heart problems. Flunarazine is considered safe, except for use in Parkinson's patients and in people who have mental depression. Flunarazine is used more frequently than any other calcium channel blocker.

Common side effects include drowsiness, especially at the start of treatment, but this gradually improves. Weight gain may be a problem with the use of flunarazine, as may strange, uncontrolled movements of the arms and legs. Patients are also advised to practise good oral hygiene, as this medication may cause bleeding, tender gums.

If any side effects worsen with time or become increasingly bothersome, you should see your doctor. Do not stop taking your medicine without first consulting your doctor or pharmacist.

> Examples of calcium channel blockers used to prevent migraines:
>
> Flunarazine (Sibelium®)
>
> Verapamil (Isoptin®)

ALPHA AGONISTS

Clonidine acts on certain receptors, called alpha-receptors, in the smooth muscle tissues of blood vessels. This prevents blood vessels from suddenly narrowing and dilating. Thereby it inhibits a migraine attack form occurring. It is a safe medication, especially because it is used at a very low dosage in migraine treatment. It is usually used in those patients who get migraines from certain foods containing a substance called tyramine, which is a known trigger factor for migraine headaches. It seems to work well for certain patients, even though it is not considered to be the most effective medication for migraine prevention.

Clonidine is taken as a twice to three times daily dosage, and if there has been no improvement of migraine attacks in two to four weeks, then the dosage may need to be doubled. Even then, the dosage is still considered to be low.

There are very few side effects, and those that may occur only do so in very few patients. Side effects include dizziness, drowsiness, dry mouth, skin rashes, impotence, depression, and fainting when getting up rapidly from a sitting or lying down position. These effects are seldom seen, and are more predominant in hot weather, where blood vessels will already be dilated in order to help the body cool off.

Alcohol and sleeping pills may interact with clonidine, causing drowsiness.

Clonidine has been shown to be only moderately effective in migraine prevention, but can prevent migraine recurrence even long after the therapy has been discontinued. If therapy needs to be discontinued, remember to do so only with your doctor's approval, and to do so slowly. If you are also taking a beta-blocker or tricyclic antidepressant together with clonidine, then you need to be cautious about ending your therapy, as you can develop unwanted withdrawal effects, such as very high blood pressure, which can be dangerous. Speak to your doctor or pharmacist when you are contemplating discontinuing your medication.

A favorable advantage in taking clonidine is that it prevents hot flushes, so it may be a good choice for a migraine sufferer who tends to blush a lot, especially if this brings on migraine attacks. Blushing or flushing usually occurs because blood vessels are stimulated to suddenly widen, making the person feel hot and red. Some sufferers may be quite sensitive to this kind of reaction, especially when stressed. It is sometimes used in menopausal women to prevent hot flushes, so a menopausal woman suffering from migraines may find this medication quite useful.

Examples of alpha agonists used to treat migraines:

Clonidine (Dixarit®)

ANTI-EPILEPTICS

A relatively new trend in the prevention of migraines is the use of certain anti-epileptic medicines such as topiramate. The theory behind the use of these medicines is that migraines can be similar in nature to epilepsy, due to overactive nerve impulses in the brain.

These medicines have only just recently been approved for use in the prevention of migraines. Until recently, they were prescribed purely at the discretion of the prescribing doctor. They have been employed in the prevention of migraines in certain cases, often when none of the other treatments or preventative measures have been successful. The exact mode of action of anti-epileptic medicines in migraines is as yet not fully understood.

Some patients have experienced marked relief from their pain, whereas others have noticed little change. The prescribing regimen is started at a low dose, and is increased gradually until the correct and therapeutic level has been reached. These medicines are taken daily to produce enough of a concentration in the body in order to prevent the onset of a migraine headache, and are not to be used for the treatment of an acute migraine attack. Withdrawal of this medicine should likewise follow a very gradual pattern, so as not to produce unwanted adverse effects. Do not at any stage stop taking these medicines without the advice of your doctor.

Anti-epileptic medicines are traditionally coupled by fairly severe side effects, and they tend to interact with a multitude of other medicines used for treating other illnesses, as well as numerous medical conditions. Interacting medicines include certain antibiotics, tricyclic antidepressants, other anti-epileptic medicines, sedatives, digoxin, some diuretics, certain oral anti-diabetic medicines, lithium, and oral contraceptives, among others. Remember also that numerous herbal supplements may interact with anti-epileptic medicines. Just because they are herbal or natural does not necessarily mean that these supplements are safe or harmless.

Make sure that your doctor is fully aware of all medicines you are taking before prescribing an anti-epileptic for your migraines, and likewise inform a doctor of the fact that you are being prescribed an anti-epileptic, should you require medication to treat a subsequent complaint. Some of the drug interactions can have severe consequences.

If you are pregnant, wanting to become pregnant, or you are breastfeeding, then it may be a better idea to discontinue therapy with topiramate under your doctor's supervision, as it can lead to problems. Discus this issue carefully with your doctor so that you can decide on a safer and more favorable alternative.

Side effects include tiredness, weakness, confusion, nervousness, dizziness, visual and speech disturbances, menstrual changes, appetite and weight loss, tingling arms and legs, memory problems, and metabolic acidosis, which can lead to heart palpitations, hyperventilation, and kidney stones, among others. Should you experience strange side effects, please speak to your doctor immediately, and voice your concerns before discontinuing treatment. The incidence of side effects increases with increased dosage. Your doctor will therefore gradually increase your dosage to prevent these adverse reactions, but should you start experiencing them, then mention them as soon as possible.

Apart from topiramate, other anti-epileptic medicines have also been used "off-label" to prevent migraines. This book, therefore, does not mention these medicines which have not yet been registered for this purpose. Some have produced favorable results in patients, but sometimes the risks of adverse reactions or concurrent medical conditions will make these medicines unsuitable for use in many patients. If you are on a regimen of this type, then please refer any questions or concerns to your prescribing doctor, as you will obtain the most relevant advice directly from him or her.

These medicines have given promise to some who have tried many other cures unsuccessfully. They are a useful alternative and should be considered if you suffer from severe, frequent, unrelenting, and debilitating migraines.

Examples of anti-epileptics used to treat migraines:

Topiramate (Topamax®)

CHAPTER 8

Herbal Supplements

Many herbal supplements have been used throughout the ages to treat migraines, and many have not yet undergone extensive tests and trials to prove their efficacy. They claim to be very useful in the treatment of migraines, even if their actual mode of action is not completely known or understood. However, many sufferers have found relief in some of them. Many herbal products that have historically been used to treat migraines are currently undergoing extensive trials to identify how they act, what they may interact with, their potential side effects, their optimal dosages, and how safe they are.

It is very important to note that just because a product is herbal does not mean it is always entirely safe to be used, especially if you have other medical conditions or if you are on any other medication. Herbal remedies do have the potential to interact with medicines, and some of them can make certain medical conditions worse. It is always wise to consult your doctor, pharmacist, or alternative health care practitioner before you start taking an herbal supplement. In general, they can be safely used, and you may find one or more of them effective in treating or preventing your migraines. Remember that you may need to use an herbal remedy for up to three months before you see its full effect. Try not to expect results immediately, and be patient.

The only herbal supplement that is used directly to prevent migraines is feverfew. All the other herbal supplements that have been shown to be useful act indirectly to prevent migraines, by alleviating stress-related symptoms, depression, or anxiety.

FEVERFEW *(Tanacetum Parthenium)*

Feverfew is a plant belonging to the daisy family, and has been used widely for the prevention of migraines in Europe and Canada since the 1970s. It is also known as featherfew, febrifuge, or Maid's Weed.

This plant was traditionally used to cure nausea and vomiting, and has since been found to be effective in the treatment of migraines. It claims to have numerous beneficial actions, including reducing fever and inflammation and promoting restful sleep. Feverfew contains active compounds known as sesquiterpene lactones, of which the most active one is parthenolide. It is thought to reduce the production of certain mediators in the body, which cause the blood vessels to go into a spasm, thereby preventing a migraine attack. Feverfew is thought to cause the vessels to dilate, to prevent blood clotting and inhibit inflammation in the body. These actions are still being investigated.

Many sufferers have found relief in using feverfew on a daily basis to prevent migraine attacks. Feverfew is meant to reduce the frequency and severity of migraines. It cannot, however, prevent a migraine once it has begun.

Feverfew is available widely in pharmacies and health shops as a supplement. It is usually given once daily as 250 mg of feverfew with a 0.4 percent standardized parthenolide content.

Before supplements were available, the leaves of the feverfew plant used to be chewed, but this often caused mouth ulcers. Feverfew leaves can still be bought in some health shops. Feverfew should be taken after a meal to reduce unwanted side effects in the stomach.

Feverfew must be avoided in pregnancy, because it can cause the uterus to contract and thereby endanger the life of the growing fetus.

Patients taking medicines to prevent blood clotting should not take feverfew, because they may bleed excessively. Feverfew inactivates iron supplements and should be taken two hours apart.

ST. JOHN'S WORT *(Hypericum perforatum)*

St. John's wort has been used for more than 2,000 years because of its wide range of medicinal properties. This plant is thought to have been named after John the Baptist. It is frequently administered in many European countries, including Germany, the U.K., and Switzerland, and is under investigation in America and Canada for its antidepressant properties. St. John's wort can be used for numerous conditions, including anxiety, depression, sleep disorders, and even, if applied onto the skin, for burns and ulcers.

Its value in treating migraines is secondary to treating depression. St. John's wort contains various active compounds, which act together and potentiate each other's effects. Two of the many active compounds are hypericin and hyperforin. St. John's wort is thought to prevent the breakdown of certain neurotransmitters (brain chemicals), i.e. serotonin and noradrenaline. As discussed previously, an imbalance of serotonin also causes migraines. Adjusting this imbalance and furthermore treating any depression that may go hand-in-hand with migraines can prevent migraines. It is also thought to enhance the effects of a relaxing agent in the brain, called GABA (gamma amino butyric acid), thereby treating anxiety, an important trigger factor in migraines.

St. John's wort is widely available in pharmacies and health shops. A recommended dosage would be 700 mg to 900 mg of St. John's wort daily, in two to three divided doses. The hypericin content should not exceed 0.3 percent of the standardized extract. It is advisable to make sure that the product contains not only hypericin, but also the other active substances contained in St. John's wort in order to be more effective. It may take six to eight weeks for results to be shown. It is best taken after food to prevent gastric side effects, and care must be exercised to wear sunscreen while taking St. John's wort, because it can cause the skin to become sensitive to sunburn.

If you are already taking a preventative medicine for your migraines, such as tricyclic antidepressants or beta-blockers, then you should not be taking St. John's wort. St. John's wort has been shown to interact with numerous medicines, because it is broken down by the same liver enzymes as many medicines. Its use should be avoided if you are taking medicines for epilepsy (e.g. phenytoin), HIV therapy, digoxin for heart problems, asthma medicines (e.g. theophylline), cyclosporin (used to prevent organ transplant rejection), medicines to prevent blood clotting (e.g. warfarin), and the oral contraceptive pill. St. John's wort may reduce the activity of these medicines and thereby produce dangerous results. Other medicines which are frequently used to treat depression are monoamine oxidase inhibitors (MAOI, such as tranylcypromine or moclobemide) or selective serotonin re-uptake inhibitors (SSRI, such as fluoxetine, paroxetine, citalopram, or sertraline). St. John's wort should not be used concurrently with these medicines because of the risk of increasing unwanted side effects.

It should be avoided during pregnancy and breastfeeding.

Like all other substances, St. John's wort can cause certain side effects, which include constipation, dry mouth, dizziness, and sensitivity to becoming sunburned.

Speak to your health care professional before taking St. John's wort, especially if you have other medical conditions or are taking certain medicines. Also speak to your doctor or pharmacist if you are not sure whether you are taking medicines which may interact with St. John's wort. St. John's wort has been shown to be very effective in treating depression, and is often a good first choice before trying stronger antidepressants. It may well help to prevent migraines, especially if depression is associated with them.

KAVA KAVA *(Piper methysticum)*

The kava kava plant, which is related to the pepper family, was discovered in the 1770s in the South Pacific Islands, where it has been used for centuries in the treatment of anxiety, tension, and sleeplessness, as well as urinary tract infections, arthritis, and breathing disorders. It used to be brewed as a calming tea, but is nowadays available in tablet form. It is frequently prescribed in Europe for anxiety, including anxiety attacks, sleeplessness, stress, tension, aggression, depression, and restlessness. Recently it has been found to be useful in preventing migraines because of its relaxant properties. Muscle tension, stress, depression, and anxiety are definite migraine trigger factors, and by eliminating them, migraines can be prevented. Kava kava instills a sense of peace into the patient and has a rapid calming action. Results are evident immediately.

Kava kava contains numerous active substances, among which are the kavalactones. There are different types of kavalactones, but they all work best when taken together, as they enhance each other's effects. These chemicals seem to act on a substance in the brain called GABA (gamma amino butyric acid), which makes the body relax.

Kava kava can be safely taken with almost any other supplement or medicine, but caution must be exercised in patients suffering from Parkinsonism, depression, and liver disease. It should also be avoided in pregnancy. People taking anti-epileptic medicines or sedatives should likewise only use kava kava if their doctor has allowed it. Kava kava is taken up to three times daily in order to exert its relaxing effect. It does not, however, cause sedation, drowsiness, or confusion, so it can safely be taken during the day, as long as dosage recommendations are observed.

The recommended dosage of kava kava is usually 250 to 300 mg of a 30 percent standardized extract twice to three times daily. The extract should contain a blend of kavalactones in order to be more effective.

Side effects are rare, but include dry, scaly skin, stomach complaints, labored breathing, and, with long-term use, jaundice (yellowing of the skin due to liver damage).

Many sufferers have claimed that their migraines have improved while using kava kava; however, it should not be used on an ongoing basis for more than a few weeks at a time, because of its ability to affect the liver.

CHAPTER 9

Helpful Vitamins and Minerals

MAGNESIUM

Magnesium is known as the anti-stress mineral. This action in itself is useful in treating migraines, because of treating the stress component. It has been known to help in the treatment of mild depression, which is often associated with migraines. In addition, it relaxes tense muscles, prevents muscle cramps, and promotes health in the heart and blood vessels. Blood vessels are very much involved in migraines, as are tense muscles. Magnesium has often been prescribed in a treatment regimen for migraines, because of its potential to aid in migraine control.

There are numerous natural sources of magnesium, such as seeds and nuts, dark green vegetables such as spinach, and certain fruits such as apples, citrus fruits, and figs.

It is widely available as a mineral supplement, often in combination with calcium, with which it maintains a subtle balance in the body. Too much magnesium on its own can cause diarrhea, so it is often advisable to take calcium together with it, to prevent this. Calcium is often referred to as "nature's tranquilizer," which can help to reduce stress levels and aid in more restful sleep. Therefore it too can have favorable effects on migraines.

Magnesium is available in a variety of different dosage forms, ranging from liquids and tablets to powders and effervescent drinks. Magnesium also exists as a slow release formulation, and this makes dosing easy, as only one capsule is needed daily. The magnesium is released over numerous hours, which benefits the body for a longer period of time. Magnesium in some products is attached to a protein, i.e. it is chelated, which enables it to be more readily absorbed into the body. This ensures that more magnesium is absorbed, and allows for more effective treatment. Magnesium supplements should be taken for three months for results to become evident. Dolomite is an inexpensive supplement, containing both magnesium and calcium in the correct proportions, but at a relatively low dosage. This should be taken three times daily, preferably with meals, to enhance absorption.

Alcohol, water pills, and hormonal contraceptive pills tend to decrease magnesium levels in the body, so supplementation may be required.

VITAMIN B

There are numerous vitamins in the vitamin B family. Generally it is better to take a vitamin B complex (combination of many of the B vitamins) than any one of the vitamin B family on its own, because they work together and enhance each other's actions. Vitamin B complex is known as an anti-stress complex, because it helps to alleviate stress and helps the body to fight off fatigue during times of stress. Vitamin B2 (riboflavin), especially, has been recommended for use in migraine sufferers, mainly because of its abilities to help the body cope with stress. Vitamin B3 (niacin) has been said to be effective in the treatment of migraines, because it improves blood circulation. Vitamin B6 (pyridoxine) has been known to have anti-depressant activity. Vitamin B1 (thiamine), vitamin B6, and folic acid, which is also a B vitamin, are all known to maintain a healthy nervous system.

As mentioned before, migraines are often accompanied by depression, caused or exacerbated by stress, and pre-empted by disturbances in blood circulation, leading to the belief that vitamin B can help in the treatment of migraines. B vitamins should be taken daily for two to three months in order for their effects to be noticeable in the management of migraines.

B vitamins are water-soluble, and hence need to be replaced on a daily basis. B vitamins are not stored by the body. The body absorbs as much as it needs and eliminates the rest. This is why people who take a lot of B vitamins will find that their urine will be bright yellow in color. The excess vitamin B that is not used will be excreted in the urine and give it its yellow color.

During times of stress, the need for the B vitamins increases, as the body uses more of them. Smokers, chronically ill people, heavy consumers of alcohol, patients on antidepressants and isoniazid (tuberculosis medication), pregnant women, and women on the oral contraceptive pill also have higher vitamin B requirements.

Natural sources of B vitamins are green vegetables (e.g. peas, spinach, broccoli), beans and lentils, fruit (e.g. avocados, dates, prunes, bananas), eggs, nuts, wheat germ, brewer's yeast, fish, red meat, and poultry. In addition, there are many vitamin B supplements available on the market, ranging from tablets to capsules to effervescent tablets. There are some slow-release supplements available, which are released over eight hours, thereby increasing the benefit of the vitamins.

Vitamin B supplements are best taken in the morning, because they aid in fighting fatigue, and could, in sensitive people, affect sleeping patterns.

B vitamins can interact with certain medicines, such as diabetic medicines or insulin, certain cholesterol-lowering agents, some cancer chemotherapy (i.e. methotrexate), and anti-Parkinson's medicines (i.e. levodopa). Consult your doctor or pharmacist if you are taking any of these medicines and want to use B vitamins.

B vitamins are safe in pregnancy, but dosage instructions must be observed.

OMEGA-3 ESSENTIAL FATTY ACIDS

Omega-3 fatty acids have been found to be very useful in reducing the severity and frequency of migraines. They are thought to prevent the inflammation and smooth muscle spasms in the blood vessels of the brain, both of which are implicated in migraine headaches. These are only two of the many other benefits of the omega-3 fatty acids, which possibly include improving depression, which often accompanies migraines.

Omega-3 fatty acids are essential in the body, as the human body does not produce these fatty acids internally. Omega-3 and omega-6 fatty acids work together in the body to keep it healthy. They act on similar pathways, but produce opposing results, thereby achieving a balance. Their primary action is in the production of prostaglandins, which are hormone-like substances that act as messengers and catalysts in many of the body's functions. Some prostaglandins produce a protective inflammation in the body, which helps to identify when there is a problem. Other prostaglandins produce an anti-inflammatory effect, thereby helping the body to heal itself.

In balance, this works exceptionally well. The optimal ratio of omega-6 to omega-3 should be 1:2. However, omega-6 fatty acids, unlike omega-3 fatty acids, are usually consumed in sufficient quantities in our daily diets in vegetable and plant oils. The modern Western diet lacks sufficient intake of omega-3 fatty acids, and this ratio is thereby vastly disturbed. This can then give rise to many inflammatory conditions, including arthritis, cardiovascular problems—which includes inflammation of blood vessels (such as in migraines), ulcerative colitis, asthma, eczema, and many more. Therefore, the supplementation of omega-3 fatty acids is much more important than that of omega-6 fatty acids. If one pathway is excessive, then it becomes dominant and can produce unwanted symptoms.

The derivatives of omega-3 fatty acids are very important in the anti-inflammatory processes in the body. These derivatives are eicosapentanoic acid (EPA) and docosahexanoic acid (DHA). They help in the production of beneficial prostaglandins, as well as in the development of the nervous system, brain, and eyes. Omega-3 fatty acids and derivatives are found mainly in fatty or oily fish, such as salmon, tuna, mackerel, and sardines, as well as in linseeds. Deep water fish eat plankton, which contains omega-3 fatty acids. The deeper and colder the water, the higher the omega-3 content in the plankton, and therefore the higher the content in the fish. By eating more of these fish and also linseeds, the body can be naturally supplemented with omega-3 fatty acids.

There are many supplements available on the market in the form of capsules. To prevent migraines, an optimal supplement would be to take cold water salmon oil capsules, with a high content of DHA and EPA. Start off by taking two 1,000-mg capsules three times daily for a month to build up the omega-3 levels in the body and allow for it to start acting. Then reduce to 1,000 mg three times daily. This will aid in nerve transmission and anti-inflammatory effects, and can thereby reduce the frequency and severity of migraines. Buy a good-quality product and store it in a fridge, as fatty acids can go rancid if exposed to heat and light. Take them at meals to improve absorption and prevent possible side effects such as bloating, flatulence, diarrhea, nausea, and burping. Sometimes an unwanted reaction is a fishy body odor, but if this occurs, then try a different product before stopping supplementation. If it persists, then change to linseed oil instead. Be aware that cod liver oil is not advisable, because it contains high quantities of vitamins A and D, which can be harmful in excess. The omega-3 content is too low in cod liver oil capsules compared to the content of vitamins A and D.

There are many benefits in taking omega-3 fatty acids. It is generally safe for use, even in pregnancy and breastfeeding, where it can have beneficial results on the baby, as it has been thought to increase intelligence, improve nerve conduction, and help in the development of the nervous system, brain, and eyes. It can also aid in strengthening the immune system and prevent allergies. In the elderly, it can help arthritis, reduce blood cholesterol, and protect the cardiovascular system. It is thought to promote mental health, as well as help in depression, PMS, cancer, liver disorders, and skin conditions, among many other conditions.

However, diabetic and epileptic patients should not supplement with omega-3 fatty acids without the approval of their specialist. Omega-3 fatty acids can affect blood sugar balance and may also interfere with anti-epileptic medicines. Caution should be exercised in patients taking anti-clotting medicines such as warfarin, heparin, and low-dose aspirin, as blood clotting can be inhibited too much and produce bleeding.

TRIMETHYLGLYCINE (TMG)

Some years ago, it was discovered that a certain amino acid is produced in the body called homocysteine. This is a harmful and destructive amino acid, which is produced by the body because of a genetic predisposition, or even during certain illnesses and extreme stress. Homocysteine increases the chance of inflammatory diseases, cardiovascular illnesses, and stress-related conditions. First and foremost, homocysteine is researched in the cardiovascular circles, because it is a well-known indicator of heart disease, stroke, and harmful cholesterol. In reducing the body's levels of homocysteine, bad cholesterol can be reduced, incidences of heart disease and stroke can be avoided, inflammatory illness can be reduced, and stress can be alleviated to some degree. Simple urine and blood tests can be performed to check the levels of homocysteine in the body.

As migraines have a large cardiovascular component, as well as a stress component to them, it would stand to reason that homocysteine levels may well be elevated in migraine sufferers, and that migraines could be controlled by reducing the body's homocysteine levels. A fair amount of research has gone into trying to prove that migraine sufferers have elevated homocysteine levels, and some results have indeed shown this to be the case. As different migraine sufferers have varying trigger factors for their migraines, it would possibly mean that the levels of homocysteine are not necessarily elevated for all sufferers. It is thought that people who suffer from migraines with aura are more likely to have elevated homocysteine levels. Therefore, it would be well worth a try for migraine sufferers to have their homocysteine levels analyzed in order to establish whether they are high.

The reduction of homocysteine in the body is very simple. All it requires is the intake of certain vitamins in the correct proportions and some dietary modifications. It has been found that a combination of various B vitamins with trimethylglycine (TMG), folic acid, zinc, and magnesium can effectively reduce the levels of destructive homocysteine. There are various combination products available which contain some or most of these vitamins in one preparation. Otherwise a strong vitamin B complex, containing vitamins B2, B6, B12, and folic acid can be taken together with zinc and magnesium, which are also widely available. TMG is probably the most important component in the reduction of homocysteine levels. Should a combination of B vitamins and folic acid not produce satisfactory reductions in homocysteine, then TMG should be added. TMG has three methyl groups attached to it, which serve to deactivate harmful homocysteine. It also protects the liver, helps with detoxification of the liver, and can aid in cellular repair processes. If TMG cannot be obtained, then other alternatives would be the intake of choline or lecithin, which also act as methyl donors in the deactivation of homocysteine. These would not be a first choice, but will do in the absence of TMG. TMG is also sometimes referred to as betaine, and this is usually available as betaine hydrochloride. Betaine hydrochloride seems to be mainly marketed to people who suffer from low levels of stomach acid, so do not be surprised if the label mentions this as its primary function.

The amount of TMG necessary to reduce homocysteine varies from 500 mg to 3,000 mg daily, depending on how high the levels are per individual. If you start on a high dose of TMG, then have regular check-ups to establish whether your homocysteine levels are being reduced and whether you should be taking a lower dosage of TMG. Only take as much as you really need to avoid potential adverse reactions.

Dietary modifications should include the reduction of fatty foods and limited intake of salt, alcohol, and caffeine. Diets should be rich in fresh fruit, legumes, beets, and vegetables. Water intake should be around two liters a day for adults. It has also been found that a clove of garlic a day seems to be beneficial. Some sources advocate the substitution of red meat with fish in order to reduce homocysteine in the body.

To date, there do not seem to be any recorded interactions with TMG and other medicines on the market. Should you be considering supplementing with TMG and you are currently taking other medicines, then refer to your doctor, pharmacist, or health care provider in order to check whether they approve of your taking it. It has not been studied in pregnancy and during breastfeeding, so it would be safer to avoid during these times, just in case. It is unlikely to be a problem, but as it has not been proven safe, it should best be avoided.

Excessive levels of TMG can cause headaches and nausea as a side effect. Therefore, establish what your levels of homocysteine are before supplementing.

Numerous books have been written on this topic and are available in the bookstores for further study. TMG looks as though it has great potential in the reduction of migraines in some sufferers. It is a very safe supplement, with few adverse effects and interactions. Therefore, it is definitely worth considering if you are at a loss of what to do about your pain.

As TMG is a natural supplement, it may take up to two weeks for its effects to be noticeable. Give it at least that time, but preferably more than that. TMG would be especially beneficial in migraine sufferers who are also battling with high stress, elevated cholesterol levels, atherosclerosis, and who have a history of cardiac disease in the family. Some sources say that it may even help with thyroid deficiencies, perhaps osteoporosis, and that it may even have anti-aging benefits. As noted before, mention this to your physician before starting on a regimen if you have any pre-existing conditions or are taking other medicines.

CHAPTER 10

Alternative Therapies

There are many alternative therapies available that claim to be effective in treating and preventing migraines. Some of these natural remedies have undergone testing, whereas with others the claims are still unsubstantiated.

Just because a cure is natural does not necessarily mean that it is completely safe. Natural remedies can still harmfully affect pregnant women, cause skin allergies and sun sensitivity, result in side effects, and interact dangerously with other medicines and medical conditions.

Very often, natural or alternative remedies work very well in conjunction with conventional therapies. If the therapies do not interact with each other, the patient can be more holistically healed. It is important to note that if the new alternative therapy tends to interact with an existing medical treatment for an existing medical condition, then the alternative therapy should be discontinued, not the existing medical treatment. This could otherwise lead to life-threatening circumstances, depending on what the condition is that is being treated.

It is advisable to speak to your doctor, pharmacist, homeopath, or alternative practitioner before using an alternative remedy to ensure that it is used safely and correctly.

HOMEOPATHY

A German doctor, Samuel Hahnemann, who found that some conventional medical practices at that time were rather extreme in treating illnesses, developed homeopathy in the eighteenth century. He began testing certain remedies on himself, and thereby learned which substances caused which effects.

Homeopathic remedies treat an ailment with small quantities of natural extracts. These treatments generally exist as powders, tinctures (alcoholic mixtures), or pilules (tiny, round sugar pills onto which the active ingredient is sprayed). Homeopathy believes in treating like with like, i.e. it uses highly diluted substances, which if taken in a large quantity, will produce exactly the symptoms you are suffering from. Homeopathy works by stimulating the immune system, thereby giving the body the ability to fight the symptoms on its own and heal itself. Remedies are described according to the symptoms they would cause if taken in excessive amounts.

Homeopathic remedies are meant to treat the body holistically, which means that all symptoms and personal characteristics will be taken into account before any cure is prescribed. Because of this, there is no single migraine treatment available that works for every sufferer. The homeopath will take a detailed personal history, including lifestyle, personality, external influences, signs, and symptoms, and then decide which remedy will suit you best. Make sure that you take it exactly as directed to obtain maximum benefit. Remedies should generally be taken on an empty stomach and nothing should be ingested for at least fifteen minutes after a dose. Homeopathy is usually safe, but check with a practitioner if you have any additional conditions. Some herbal and aromatherapeutic remedies may interact with homeopathic treatments, and it is therefore wise to consult someone who is trained in homeopathic principles before taking too many alternative therapies together.

During a migraine attack, some remedies can be used every fifteen minutes until the pain subsides, then three times daily.

Homeopathic medicines that are known to be effective in treating migraines are:

Belladonna

This can be used for a pain that occurs generally on the right-hand side of the face, often resulting in that cheek being very flushed, hot, and red. Belladonna helps when the pain is a throbbing one or is sensitive to light, noise, and movement. It is a severe, drumming headache, which seems to appear suddenly.

Aconite

This is used for a pain that forms a band over the whole head and seems to crush the skull. Nausea is associated with this pain. Aconite is sometimes used interchangeably with belladonna.

Bryonia

This can be used when an intense, bursting headache is aggravated by movement. Associated symptoms are usually a dry mouth and thirst. Applying pressure to the face and neck can additionally relieve pain.

Natrium Muriaticum

This is used for a throbbing, blinding headache, which starts in the morning and gets worse throughout the day. The pain seems to cause numbness. The skull feels as though it is being compressed. Cold packs often come in useful in combination with this therapy.

Gelsemium

The pain experienced for this remedy is a dull, throbbing headache, radiating from the base of the skull into a viselike pressure over the head. The head is sensitive to touch, and there is weakness in the arms and legs. The patient often feels cold.

Iris Versicolor

This remedy is useful in a migraine, which begins with blurred vision, nausea, and vomiting up of bile. Associated symptoms are weakness, a tight scalp, feverishness, and tiredness. Cold compresses may prove to be useful.

Sepia

This can be used in a pain radiating from the left eye to the base of the scalp. Associated symptoms are lack of hunger, aversion to food, and tiredness.

It is best to consult a homeopath who can prescribe a specific migraine remedy for you. Some homeopathic companies prepare a general migraine formulation for sufferers which contain many of these remedies. They may also contain *Nux Vomica*, which is useful in treating nausea. These drops tend to be effective, as they cover the whole spectrum of migraines, but are less specific than those prepared specially by a homeopath.

A homeopath may identify that an organ in your body, e.g. the liver, is not well and is causing your migraines. Therapies may therefore be prescribed to treat the ailing organ in addition to migraine remedies. You may therefore find that your treatment will be more successful if you visit a homeopath, rather than self-medicating.

TISSUE SALTS

It is believed that there are twelve inorganic tissue salts which are vitally important in the body and which determine the healthy functioning of cells and tissues. If there is an imbalance of one or more tissue salts in the body, then the deprived organs or tissues, which depend on those salts for healthy functioning, will produce certain symptoms. As soon as the lacking tissue salts are supplied to the ailing body, healthy functions will be re-established, and symptoms will be cured. In migraines, there are four tissue salts which are thought to be imbalanced in the body, namely mag phos, ferrum phos, kali phos, and nat sulph.

Mag Phos

The two elements which make up this salt are magnesium and phosphorus. This salt is involved with the healthy functioning of the nerves in the body. If it is imbalanced, then it can cause cramps and shooting nerve pains in the head, face, stomach, and other parts of the body. It can be given in hot water every hour for an acute migraine attack.

Ferrum Phos

This salt is made up of iron and phosphorus. A deficiency in this salt is said to give rise to all inflammatory conditions in the body, including a throbbing, tender headache, associated with nausea and vomiting.

Kali Phos

The constituents of this salt are calcium and phosphorus. It is meant to be the most potent nerve and brain remedy of all the tissue salts. It is said to cure all nerve-related ailments, including dizziness due to nervous exhaustion, depression, bad breath, and even paralysis. It is effective for stress-related sleeplessness and headache, especially radiating from the base of the head.

Nat Sulph

Sodium and sulfur make up this salt, which is said to be useful in treating headaches radiating from the top of the skull and base of the head, especially if it is associated with nausea, vomiting, and dizziness.

Tissue salts are widely available in pharmacies and health shops. They are safe to use, but always check with your health care professional before taking a natural remedy to ensure that you are using it correctly and that it does not interfere with any other treatment or medical condition.

AROMATHERAPY

Aromatherapy has been in use since the ancient Egyptians, who already saw the benefits to using essential oils as therapy for numerous ailments. Since then, this type of treatment has been refined and perfected, and is used widely these days as an alternative remedy.

Aromatherapy oils can be used and applied in various ways. A few drops can be added to a bath, a steam inhalation, or even a suitable aromatherapy burner. Alternatively, a compress can be made by soaking a cloth in water which has had aromatherapy oils added to it, and this can be applied to the head, temples, or back of the neck for the treatment of migraines. Massage is another method of applying healing oils to the body, but care must be taken not to apply the oils to the skin in concentrated form. The oils need to be diluted with a suitable carrier oil, such as Evening Primrose oil, sweet almond oil, grapeseed, or wheat germ oil. Aromatherapy massage is a very effective method of treating migraines, because it incorporates the use of relaxing massage therapy with the administration of soothing oils. Massage also ensures that the body's circulation is improved and can enhance absorption of a healing oil into the blood.

Although they are generally safe to use, care must be taken in pregnancy, with very young children, and in people who have sensitive skins. Some essential oils can cause allergic reactions or make the patient more sensitive to becoming sunburned. Asthmatics and epileptic patients should only use aromatherapy with the approval of their doctor. Always check with your health care practitioner whether it is safe for you to use a particular aromatherapy oil.

For migraines, numerous oils have been found to be useful. Those include lavender, peppermint, grapefruit, and marjoram oils.

Lavender *(Lavendula augustifolia)*

This is a soothing oil known to help with stress and anxiety. It may also help with sleeplessness. Lavender is a popular therapy used in treating migraines. It has been included in

Migrasticks®, which apply a blend of useful oils via a roller-ball action to the temples. It is also available in numerous bath products, i.e. bubble baths, bath oils, and bath salts, which are potentially very useful methods of helping with migraines, because they use lavender oil delivered in a soothing medium. Be sure not to make your bath too hot, if you should use these methods of administering lavender, as heat can cause vasodilation and thereby exacerbate an existing migraine or cause a new one. Lavender should be avoided in the first three months of pregnancy.

Peppermint *(Mentha piperita)*

This strong-smelling oil is of a more stimulating nature, and may be useful at the end of a migraine to promote recovery. It can also be helpful if there is overlapping sinus congestion, because of its decongestant (opening of the nasal passages) action. Peppermint oil should be avoided in pregnancy, and it may cause skin allergies in sensitive people. It can also potentially interact with homeopathic remedies.

Grapefruit *(Citrus paradisi)*

This aromatherapy remedy has an uplifting and revitalizing action, especially at times of stress and nervous exhaustion. It may cause skin allergies, and can make the skin more sensitive to sunburn.

Marjoram *(Origanum marjorana)*

This oil's warm, spicy scent makes it popular, because of its comforting, soothing effect on the body. It tends to help relax tired muscles. Tiredness, muscle tension, and stress can aggravate a migraine or cause one. This oil may therefore be useful in migraines. Marjoram is not safe during pregnancy and should be avoided.

Aromatherapy has been shown, in numerous studies, to be very effective as an adjunctive treatment to many medical conditions, and can improve a sufferer's sense of well-being.

REFLEXOLOGY

Reflexology has been used in China for about 5,000 years, and is often combined with Chinese theories on body energy zones, called meridians. Each area of the foot represents a different organ or part of the body. The big toe seems to correspond with the head, and is usually the part massaged in the treatment of migraines. The outer side of the foot represents the spine and neck, and is also often manipulated during migraine therapy. A reflexologist will be able to identify problem areas in the body from merely looking at the appearance of the foot, and also through watching the reactions of the patient when stimulating a sensitive area. In some cases, the hand is used for reflexology massages instead of the foot.

Reflexology principles are not completely understood, but they are known to be effective in the treatment of many disorders, especially those related to stress and tension. Massages can induce relaxation in a person and improve general well-being. It can, however, cause some discomfort, especially on a first visit or if there is an underlying medical condition. Sometimes the triggering of certain energy zones can cause side effects, such as headaches, fatigue, or restlessness.

Regular visits tend to be effective in treating migraines. Whether this is because of the deep relaxation induced by the massage or because of hitting the correct problem area is not completely known. However, reflexology remains a very popular alternative therapy to treating migraines, and is worth trying if you do not want to take medication. A reflexologist can alleviate migraine attacks as they occur, or prevent migraines altogether by manipulating the big toe and other sensitive areas on the foot. It is important to drink plenty of water after a reflexology massage, in order to eliminate unwanted toxins and to get some rest.

Aromatherapy oils are frequently used during a foot massage, to further help in dealing with various problems.

Reflexology seems to be a fairly harmless therapy, but it is nevertheless a good idea to inform your reflexologist if you have any underlying medical conditions.

ACUPUNCTURE AND ACUPRESSURE

Acupuncture has been practised in China for more than 3,000 years. The theory behind acupuncture is that there are twelve meridians in the body which are life energy channels. The energy that flows through these channels is referred to as "qi." These meridians are named after different organs in the body, e.g. the heart or liver meridian. The undisturbed flow of qi through these channels is meant to be essential for good health. If one or more of these channels is blocked, then there will be certain symptoms and illness. There are about 365 acupoints in the body where this energy can enter or leave the body, and it is at these points that an acupuncturist will insert a needle. The method of inserting the needle determines whether the energy flow is increased, decreased, or stabilized.

Acupuncture has been used in anesthesia in China. It is thought to release the body's natural painkillers, called endorphins. Acupuncture seems to be extremely effective in treating all types of pain, even migraines. Western doctors appreciate its effectiveness, although the theory of body meridians and the disruption of qi in these channels are not well understood.

Many sufferers who have tried acupuncture have found that their migraine frequency and severity have improved. It is meant to be a deeply relaxing therapy, which in itself can help to treat stress-related migraines. The acupuncturist will ask numerous questions to identify which meridian is affected and is causing your migraine before inserting any needles. Make sure that your acupuncturist is qualified, as the technique is a very sensitive and delicate one. Avoid acupuncture during pregnancy. Heavy exercise, large meals, alcohol, and hot baths should best be avoided before a session, as these may counteract the effects of the therapy.

For those who fear needles, there is a therapy called "acupressure," which is thought to be the predecessor of acupuncture. Acupressure involves the stimulation of the acupoints with hands, fingers, feet, and knees, instead of needles. The pressure exerted on the acupoints ranges from very light and gentle to fairly intense. It is less invasive than acupuncture, but its effectiveness in the depth of stimulation may be slightly reduced. One advantage to acupressure is that you can be taught to self-administer treatment from home. There are numerous acupressure points in the face, along the neck and shoulders, and at back of the head, which, even when self-stimulated, provide almost immediate relief from pain. These points are easy to find, and your therapist can show them to you for your own use. In addition, there are migraine acupressure points in the hands and feet. When relatively high pressure is applied in the correct area, pain subsides. It is often easier to locate the acupressure points on the hand, which proves very useful for self-stimulation if in a public area. The tip of the toe also has an effective acupoint, and a therapist will often wiggle the toe and massage its tip for migraine treatment.

In general, acupuncture and acupressure have been shown to be very effective in the management of pain, and could play an important role in treating and preventing migraine headaches.

MASSAGE

Massage has been known to be effective for centuries, with even Julius Caesar receiving regular massage therapy for his headaches. Massage of the head, temples, neck, shoulders, and back can be tremendously effective in relieving discomfort. Massage stimulates blood flow to an area and helps to relax tense muscles. The skin has many sensors which are stimulated by touch, and these can induce the release of natural painkillers in the body, called endorphins. Another positive feature is that the sufferer is made to relax during the time of a massage.

Massage has been proven to be very beneficial in the treatment of numerous illnesses and conditions, including migraine headaches. Massage boosts the immune system and enhances blood circulation and lymph drainage, thereby encouraging the removal of metabolic wastes; aids in digestive problems; can reduce blood pressure and heart rate; and can promote a greater sense of health and well-being. Studies have shown that patients who receive regular massages, whether or not in addition to medication, feel more relaxed, less stressed, and have a more positive self-image. Many alternative therapies incorporate some form of massage into their treatment regimens, e.g. aromatherapy, Ayurveda (traditional Indian medicine), and reflexology.

Physiotherapists manipulate the muscles that are strained or are in spasm, and thereby help to alleviate migraines caused through tension. Many clinics offer Indian head massages, in which the therapist concentrates purely on the muscles of the head. Massage can be self-administered, but this is not as relaxing and therefore not as beneficial as having another person perform the massage. If you do massage yourself, be careful to avoid pressurizing bruises, boils, swellings, or injuries.

Self-massage can provide some relief if you are unable to see a massage therapist at the time of a migraine attack. By massaging your temples and head in circular motions with your fingers, blood circulation to the area will improve, often exhibited by a warm, tingling sensation. Likewise, by inserting the thumbs into the hollows at the base of the head and massaging in deep, circular motions, pain can be relieved to some extent. Speak to your massage therapist to show you how best to administer a massage to yourself during a migraine.

Although massage is generally safe, caution should be exercised in the first trimester of pregnancy, during infection when there is a fever, and with certain blood clotting problems. Check with your doctor about having a massage if you do suffer from a blood clotting problem or from varicose veins. Its benefits are so well accepted that it definitely is worth a try, especially if your migraines seem to be related to stress, muscle tension, and anxiety.

Regular massages have proven to be beneficial in the treatment of so many illnesses, including asthma and cancer, that it has become an increasingly popular alternative remedy to stress-related or stress-exacerbated conditions. Numerous studies have been performed worldwide to show the effectiveness of massage, the most important component of which is the healing nature of human touch. This therapy is definitely worth considering in the treatment and prevention of migraine headaches.

CHIROPRACTIC

Chiropractic has only been practised for about 100 years, although spinal manipulations have been done since the days of Hippocrates. It is now one of the most popular forms of complementary medicine practised in the West.

A chiropractor will examine the entire spinal column and will also observe the patient's posture. Often sitting at a desk for long hours causes slouching, which affects general posture and can lead to pain. Chiropractors manipulate the bones in the neck and back in order to correctly reposition them. Often, a bone in the spine is just slightly misplaced, and this can cause muscle tension, discomfort, and pain, because a nerve may have become trapped or pinched. Major nerves lead from the spine to the different organs. Depending on which organ is affected, the practitioner will trace the particular nerve back to its spinal origin and check the state of the vertebrae. Many migraine sufferers find relief through chiropractic manipulations. Numerous visits to the chiropractor may be necessary at first, but spinal health can be maintained by going for regular check-ups. Sometimes a migraine may get worse after a first session at the chiropractor, but thereafter, chiropractic manipulations will help to reduce the frequency as well as the severity of migraines.

Chiropractic has been shown to be very successful in the treatment of migraines in many sufferers. However, it has little effect on some patients, probably because their migraines do not originate from a spinal problem.

Do not attempt to adjust the spinal column on your own, and do not try it on another person. The spine is quite delicate and should only be manipulated by a trained practitioner.

YOGA

Yoga has been practised since about 3000 B.C. in India, and has become very popular in the West since the 1960s. It focuses on posture and breathing exercises to relax the mind and body.

Yoga therapy uses specific positions, called *asanas,* and specific breathing exercises, called *pranayama,* to help with certain medical conditions. Yoga can be very relaxing, and this may help to sort out migraines. Your yoga therapist can advise you on positions that are known to be helpful in migraines, e.g. a shoulder stand called the cobra. This posture should help to relax the neck, head, and shoulders. It can take numerous sessions before results are evident, and you should consult with a trained yoga teacher to begin with, who can assist you with the correct methods. Practising it regularly at home will help to reduce anxiety and, hopefully, migraine attacks.

Yoga has been shown to produce favorable results in many conditions, especially in stress-related illnesses and conditions exacerbated by stress, e.g. asthma and irritable bowel disease, among others.

Yoga is generally safe to practise, but consult a therapist if you are pregnant or have circulatory or heart problems.

POSTURE MODIFYING APPLIANCE (PMA)

The Headache Clinic in South Africa has developed a device which can prevent migraines, as well as other headaches. This device is called a "posture modifying appliance" (PMA) and it has a success rate of up to 90 percent. The PMA is a small plate that is produced and fitted for each individual patient and sits against the roof of the mouth.

The theory behind the device is as follows: when stressed or tense, the tongue usually presses against palette, and this creates a certain amount of muscle tension in the mouth and therefore the jaw. This tension is then transferred to the facial muscles and hence, in response, to the muscles surrounding the head, neck and shoulders.

As these muscles tense up, a muscular migraine may result in susceptible people. The muscle tension also aggravates the larger arteries of the head, and this leads to a vascular type of migraine. Therefore, by reducing the tension in the mouth and relaxing the tongue, the migraine can be prevented.

The PMA, which is very small and inconspicuous, increases the distance between the tongue and the roof of the mouth; i.e., it places the tongue into its resting position, thereby reducing the domino effect of muscular tension around the head. All that may be required to place the tongue in its resting position is a couple of millimeters. This distance, and hence the thickness of the plate, depend on each individual patient.

A complete physical and neurological assessment is performed on each patient to determine the nature of the headache, and if there is muscle tension present then the PMA is produced. The PMA is worn continuously, even during the night while sleeping, and is only removed for eating, drinking, oral care, and contact sports. Some patients have noticed a remarkable improvement in the frequency and severity of their migraines within only a few days, whereas others may need to wear the PMA for a bit longer. It can be removed once the migraines have been alleviated. If, for some reason, the migraines recur at a later stage, then the plate can be re-introduced and worn until the migraines cease again.

This is definitely an option worth considering if you have reached your wits' end and have had enough of the suffering, especially if your migraines are frequent and debilitating. There are many advantages to using the PMA, which include the lack of adverse effects, no drug interactions, no interactions with concurrent medical conditions or illnesses, safety during pregnancy and breastfeeding, and most importantly, the provision of a long-term cure, not just short-term relief.

You can contact the Headache Clinic via the Internet at *www. headacheclinic.co.za* for further information.

CHAPTER 11

Treating Migraines in Special Cases

In this section, the treatment of migraines in special cases is discussed in some detail. The reason that these cases have deserved special mentioning is because many medicines and treatments may cause adverse and sometimes life-threatening results if used indiscriminately.

Preventative measures have not been included, because they require a doctor's prescription and are therefore administered under professional guidance. The reason for mentioning only specific remedies and treatments is because they are usually self-medicated, and professional advice is not always sought, be it from a doctor, pharmacist, or other health care provider. The list is by no means comprehensive, but deals with some of the most commonly used medicines in treating migraines.

It is imperative, should you fit into any of these categories and suffer from migraines too, that you check with your specialist as to whether he approves of you taking a certain medicine or supplement. This section should only serve as a guideline to you. If ever you are in doubt of taking a treatment, then leave it until you can obtain professional advice.

MIGRAINES IN CHILDHOOD

1. TREATMENT

Migraines can occur in children from two years of age. At this age, it is very difficult to establish that the young child has a migraine, because of the lack of ability to accurately express pain, as well as other symptoms present in migraine. Watch out for other symptoms and signs, such as light and noise sensitivity, vomiting, appetite changes, etc. You may suspect that the child has a migraine, especially if there is a family history of migraines. Make sure that a fever and a very stiff neck with the inability to touch the chin to the chest do not accompany the pain. If this should be the case, then take the child straight to the doctor. In all cases of frequent headaches lasting longer than three days in children, the child should be checked by a paediatrician to eliminate any more severe causes for head pain.

Pain:

Always start with the mildest painkiller. There is no need to overmedicate a child, if a mild painkiller will be adequate. As a first line treatment, give acetaminophen syrup. Observe the dosing instructions according to the age of the child. If there is no relief within two or three doses, then try an ibuprofen or mefenamic acid suspension. These are very effective anti-inflammatory painkillers used in young children. Try to give these to the child on a full stomach to avoid gastric irritation. If the child is vomiting and will not eat, then give mefenamic acid suppositories. These are as effective as the suspension, but will prevent affecting the empty stomach.

Should ibuprofen or mefenamic acid not work, then you can proceed to using a more potent combination product. Some may contain codeine, which is a strong painkiller, in addition to other ingredients, including acetaminophen or ibuprofen. Codeine does have a stronger painkilling action, but also has a greater side effect profile, including drowsiness and constipation. Try not to give codeine-containing products too frequently, as dependence can develop, which will have unfavourable consequences. Consequences to overusing potent painkillers are that the milder painkillers will no longer be effective, and larger, more frequent doses will be required with time. If you need to use a strong painkiller on a regular basis and for longer than three days at a time, then you should take your child to a pediatrician to be checked.

Nausea and Vomiting:

Phosphorylated sugars can be used in children of all ages. Cyclizine is another very good anti-emetic, and exists both in syrup and suppository form. Do observe dosing instructions according to the age of the child, as the suppositories are not recommended for use in children under six years of age unless the doctor has authorised their use. There are stronger anti-emetics available on prescription by the doctor, such as prochlorperazine. A very useful homeopathic alternative is nux vomica. This comes in drop form for easy dosing and can be used up to every fifteen minutes in severe nausea. It is best administered in a bit of water in children, as the drops contain alcohol, which may sting on the child's tongue.

Herbal and Natural Remedies:

In young children, it is not advisable to use potent herbal products and vitamin supplements. Most of these natural supplements do not come in pediatric dosage forms, such as syrups, suspensions, and suppositories, thereby making dosing very tricky. Giving a young child an adult dose is not recommended, as it may cause overdosing and dangerous side effects. Vitamin B syrups do exist on the market, and these can be given to the child. However, their use in children may be limited or unnecessary, as the B vitamins' main function in the treatment of migraines is stress-management. Should the child be exposed to severe stress and be of school-going age, with migraines corresponding to periods of heightened stress, then a vitamin B supplement may prove to be useful.

Omega-3 supplements will not harm the child. In fact, they may benefit the child in numerous ways, including the healthy development of the nervous system and brain. Also, these essential fatty acids will help in promoting a healthy inflammatory as well as anti-inflammatory response in the child, thereby aiding in migraine prevention. However, dosing is again problematic. Low-dose capsules can be cut in order to squeeze out the healing omega-3 oils. Some health shops stock pure linseed oil, which contains a high concentration of omega-3 fatty acid. If the child is being bottle-fed, then look for milk formulas containing DHA, which is a component of omega-3. Check with your health care practitioner that you are giving the correct dosage.

Alternative Treatments:

Alterative remedies such as homeopathy, tissue salts, aromatherapy, massage, and chiropractic may be applied to children with a large degree of success, especially because they tend to be safe and do not result in unwanted side effects. Again, consult with your qualified practitioner as to whether his trade is suitable for your particular child.

Other:

The most important method of migraine control in your child will be to monitor its diet. Keep a migraine diary for your child, and monitor which foods potentially cause migraines. This can be done, as explained previously, by eliminating known dietary trigger factors from your child's diet, and then re-introducing them one by one to assess their effect on the child's migraines. Once the trigger factors have been identified, try to avoid them as much as possible. Allow the child to have enough rest, particularly when suffering from a migraine. Darken the room and eliminate noise to aid in the treatment of a migraine. Try not to expose the child to cigarette smoke, as this can precipitate a migraine attack. Make sure that the child eats frequent, smaller meals per day, rather than one or two large ones. This will prevent the sudden drop in blood sugar, which often results in hunger headaches. Following these simple lifestyle modifications can largely control migraines. Prevention of migraines is definitely better than cure.

2. PRECAUTIONS

If the pain lasts longer than three days, if there is a fever, or if a child cannot put his or her chin to his or her chest, then take the child to a pediatrician immediately. If you are ever unsure about whether your child has a migraine or something more serious, then play it safe and take the child to a doctor. Once migraines have been diagnosed, then you should be able to self-medicate the child according to the guidelines above or the doctor's instructions.

Please note that you must never give a child under the age of fourteen years an aspirin-containing product, especially if there is a fever. Aspirin has been linked to causing a serious condition called Reye's syndrome in children, should they have a concurrent viral infection and fever when given aspirin. There are many more suitable products on the market for the treatment of pain in children.

Always observe dosing instructions when giving your child medicine. Do not overdose, as this can lead to unwanted, potentially dangerous side effects. Also, do not underdose, as the medication will be at too low a level in the body to have any desired response. Remember to always keep medicines well out of reach of children.

MIGRAINES IN PREGNANCY

---

1. TREATMENT

Pain:

Acetaminophen is viewed as the only safe painkiller. Extensive tests and research have been performed using acetaminophen in pregnancy, and it has been proclaimed to be safe. Unfortunately, many sufferers obtain little relief from acetaminophen. In cases where the migraines are so severe that the pregnant sufferer is vomiting and incapacitated for any lengths of time, the stress on the mother and unborn child may warrant stronger therapy. In this case, the doctor may use certain triptans at his discretion and with the patient's informed consent. Under no circumstances should a pregnant woman self-medicate without the prior approval of her doctor. Ergot alkaloids, for example, are very dangerous if used in pregnancy, and should be avoided in all circumstances. Anti-inflammatories, such as aspirin and ibuprofen, for example, are also unsafe in pregnancy, and should not be used unless there is doctor's prior consent.

Nausea and Vomiting:

The first choice for treating nausea and vomiting in pregnancy is a phosphorylated sugar. This is a syrup which can be taken every fifteen minutes in severe cases until the symptoms subside. Buclizine is also often used. This is a tablet which can be taken every eight hours when necessary, but may cause drowsiness. The homeopathic remedy, nux vomica, which comes in a drop form, has been used extensively in pregnant women to treat morning sickness, and may be a very useful alternative in treating the nausea and vomiting during migraines. It can be administered directly under the tongue or in a little bit of water. It may be taken up to every fifteen minutes in severe cases of nausea and vomiting until the symptoms improve.

Herbal and Natural Remedies:

Magnesium and vitamin B supplementation, within recommended doses, will not harm the fetus. Generally they will already be present in combination vitamin supplements formulated specifically for the pregnant woman. Do not take too much magnesium without balancing it with calcium.

Omega-3 fatty acids may prove to not only be useful, but also beneficial to both mother and child. Omega-3 fatty acids have anti-inflammatory properties, which have been shown to help in the treatment of migraines. In the growing fetus, they aid in promoting a healthy nervous system, brain, and eye development. If possible, supplementation should start three to six months prior to becoming pregnant.

Herbal supplements such as feverfew, kava kava, and St. John's wort should be avoided during pregnancy, because they could endanger the growing fetus. Before using any herbal or vitamin supplement in pregnancy, always check with your doctor to ensure that the product is safe. Remember that just because a supplement is "natural" or "herbal" does not necessarily mean that it is harmless or safe, especially in pregnancy. Alternative or complementary medicines do not usually undergo the same strict trials and tests as regular or allopathic medicines, and their safety in pregnancy has therefore not always been established. In pregnancy it is extremely important to contact your health care practitioner before taking any product, be it herbal, vitamin, alternative, homeopathic, or regular.

Alternative Treatments:

Some homeopathic remedies can be used, but only under the guidance of a trained homeopath. The dosage of medicaments in homeopathic preparations is very low; however, there will always be a risk. Therefore do not self-medicate, even with homeopathic remedies.

Acupuncture should be avoided, as stimulation of certain acupressure points may produce uterine contractions and, in the worst-case scenario, loss of the baby.

Tissue salts can safely be used in the prevention and cure of migraines, even during pregnancy. The addition of these salts may be beneficial to the healthy development of the fetus. Dosing instructions should be observed in all cases.

Aromatherapy may be best avoided. Certain oils such as lavender and marjoram are not safe, especially in the first trimester of pregnancy.

Reflexology can be extremely useful in pregnancy, as it not only helps to alleviate migraines, but also aids in relaxing the pregnant mother, reduces stress, and fights nausea, backache, and swollen legs. Make sure your reflexologist knows that you are pregnant, so that the stimulation of certain parts of the foot can be avoided.

Massage can be a very useful tool in relaxing a pregnant woman. It may be better to go to a registered massage therapist than to allow an unskilled person to perform a massage. Indian head massage is a good alternative remedy in the treatment of a migraine in pregnancy. Remember to warn your therapist that you are pregnant, to ensure that they do not include certain oils in your massage, such as lavender, which may be harmful to the pregnancy.

Chiropractic can alleviate migraines in pregnancy, as well as other discomforts of pregnancy, such as backache. Chiropractic for migraines is usually practised on the head, neck, and upper back. This will pose no risk to the pregnancy.

Some yoga can definitely be practised in pregnancy. However, it is important to note that you should not start doing yoga from home, if you have never practised it before your pregnancy. It will be far better for you to learn yoga under the eye of an experienced instructor, who can give you advice on which postures may benefit you, as some positions are not recommended during pregnancy. Under the care of a trained instructor, yoga can promote relaxation and improve muscle tone and breathing, and this alone can greatly benefit a pregnant migraine sufferer.

Other:

It is as important for a pregnant woman as it is with any other sufferer to observe her diet. Remember the dietary trigger factors, and attempt to avoid as many of them as possible, especially in pregnancy, when treatment becomes very complicated. It is very important to eat regular meals, to prevent hunger migraines, not only in pregnancy, but also in general. Eat five or six smaller meals a day, rather than one large one, to ensure that blood glucose levels remain constant throughout the day. Drinking two liters of water a day will help to flush out toxins, and can be beneficial in the prevention of unnecessary migraines. It is definitely better to avoid the migraine than to treat it. A pregnant woman must also get plenty of rest and try to eliminate stress factors in her life. If she can successfully manage to do this, then migraine frequency may be drastically reduced.

The good news and the glimmer of hope for all pregnant migraine sufferers is that 70 percent of women experience a marked improvement in their migraines during pregnancy. Hopefully you are part of that quota!

2. PRECAUTIONS

In pregnancy, it is always better to take as little medication as possible, because medicines can cross the placental barrier and may affect the development of the growing fetus. It is difficult to treat most illnesses with medicines in pregnancy, as most medicines will not have been tested for safety in pregnant women, as no mother would want to risk the health of her child by joining drug trials. Safety trials are performed in gestating animals, however, and through this a medicine may be viewed as potentially harmful or harmless to the human child. However, safety in pregnancy cannot generally be established precisely, as there are certain differences between the metabolisms of different mammals. The medicine's method of action in the body is also vitally important. Some medicines are known not to cross the placental barrier, as they are too large, and they therefore pose little, if any, risk to the baby.

Risk-benefit analyses will be performed in pregnant women who are very sick and require medication. If a medicine is not seen to be harmful in gestating animals and there have been cases in which pregnant women have been treated with a certain medication without any harm resulting to the unborn child, then this drug may be used in individual cases. Sometimes it is imperative to give medication to a pregnant woman, and through this the effects on the baby are examined. In some cases, a woman does not know she is pregnant, and will unwittingly have taken certain medicines. Here again, the effects of the medicine on the child can be examined. These are the main methods by which the medical fraternity can make educated decisions as to whether a medicine should or shouldn't be administered in pregnancy.

Five categories exist into which drugs for use in pregnancy are categorized. These range from Risk Factor A, where there is little if any harm to the developing child, to Risk Factor X, where there is evidence to show that the medicine will cause severe harm to the developing fetus and the medicine may not be given under any circumstances. Through this classification, it is possible to identify how dangerous the proposed treatment may be, and to act accordingly.

Herbal and natural products do not usually undergo the strict testing that regular medicine undergoes, and hence the studies into their safety in pregnancy have not always been established. Just because a product is natural, herbal, or homeopathic, does not necessarily mean that it is safe to be used during pregnancy. Therefore it is vitally important to check with your doctor, pharmacist, or alternative health care practitioner as to whether a product is safe in pregnancy before using it. If in doubt, delay in taking it until you are no longer pregnant.

MIGRAINES DURING LACTATION/ BREASTFEEDING

1. TREATMENT

Pain:

Even though your pregnancy is behind you, you still need to be careful about the medicines that you take, because some medicines will appear in your breast milk, and this will be transferred to your baby. The medicine of choice is once again acetaminophen. Acetaminophen, ibuprofen, and codeine are present in breast milk in insufficient concentrations to cause harm to the child, provided that the dosing instructions have been observed. In high doses, codeine may cause drowsiness and constipation in the baby. Aspirin is contra-indicated during breastfeeding, as it may harm the infant. Ergot alkaloids should also be avoided altogether, as they may cause severe toxic effects in the child. The triptans have not undergone sufficient research in use during breastfeeding in humans. However, animal studies show that they are present in breast milk, and manufacturers advise that breastfeeding should be withheld for twenty-four hours after taking a triptan. Contact your doctor to find out which painkiller he recommends for you to use during the time that you are breastfeeding. In times of very severe pain, you may well be given a medicine that could be potentially harmful to your suckling infant. In this case, your doctor may advise you to express milk beforehand so that you can feed the baby its breast milk from a bottle and thereby prevent putting it at risk. You may even consider using a formula for one or two feedings (you will probably need to express the unconsumed milk from your breasts to prevent engorgement and to keep up breast milk production while you are taking medicines). Ask your doctor or pharmacist how long it will take for the medicine to clear your body, so that you know when you can safely start to breastfeed your baby again.

Nausea and Vomiting:

Phosphorylated sugars are safe to use in breastfeeding. Cyclizine and buclizine may be excreted into the breast milk in small quantities, and should only be used with caution. Cyclizine and buclizine may affect milk production in the mother, and should therefore only be used if absolutely necessary. The nursing mother may choose to use homeopathic drops containing nux vomica, which are very useful in treating nausea and vomiting. These drops can be taken directly under the tongue or in a bit of water. In severe cases, the drops can be administered every fifteen minutes if necessary until the symptoms subside.

Herbal and Natural Remedies:

Large doses of vitamin B may impair the production of breast milk, so low doses are acceptable, but high doses should be avoided. Magnesium and omega-3 are safe for use in breastfeeding, and may be of benefit to both mother and child. Omega-3 will be a useful supplement to prevent migraines in the mother, and definitely has advantages when passed via the breast milk to the baby. It stimulates a healthy nervous system in the baby, and is even thought to improve a child's IQ. Numerous commercial milk formulas are fortified with essential fatty acids; therefore, fortifying breast milk with omega-3 supplements should be even better for the child.

Herbal remedies such as St. John's wort, kava kava, and feverfew should be avoided, as there is not enough information available to warrant their safety to the infant.

Alternative Treatments:

All alternative remedies are safe during breastfeeding. Caution should be exercised with the use of homeopathic remedies, and a registered homeopath should be consulted before use.

Other:

Dietary modifications are again the key to migraine prevention. As with all other cases mentioned above, it is best to use as little medication as possible in breastfeeding, to completely eliminate the possibility of harming the infant. Therefore, it is necessary to avoid a migraine wherever possible by monitoring the dietary intake of foods and drinks known to trigger migraines. None of the dietary trigger factors are essential in producing breast milk, so they can be avoided with safety. If possible, the nursing mother should try to get some rest in a darkened, quiet room in order to sleep away her pain.

2. PRECAUTIONS

Certain medicines are excreted in breast milk and can cause harmful effects on the young infant. Some medicines are present in the breast milk at such insignificant concentrations that they will not affect the baby. However, some medicines may be present at a high concentration, and may pose a risk to the child. It is important to note that there is not always sufficient evidence available through controlled studies on breastfeeding mothers, as no mother would willingly put her baby at risk. Information that is available is based on the known presence of the drug in breast milk, its concentration in the milk, and its toxicity to the child. Medicines should only be taken if necessary.

In a case when the migraine is so debilitating that the mother has to be medicated, she may want to express some milk prior to taking the medication, or she may want to take the medicines directly after a feed, to reduce the risk to the baby. It is important to remember that the mother will need to get relief from her migraine, as she will be unable to care for her infant adequately when she is suffering from such severe pain. It may even be necessary to formula-feed the infant in cases where the mother is unable to express milk, or when dosing schedules do not allow for her to prevent putting her child at risk of taking in the medication through her milk. If unsure, a call to the local pharmacist or doctor can establish the safety of a particular medication while breastfeeding.

MIGRAINES IN THE ELDERLY

1. TREATMENT

Pain:

It is always best to take the mildest effective painkiller as first-line treatment, i.e. acetaminophen. If this does not help within two or three doses, then a stronger medicine can be used. Anti-inflammatories can be risky in advancing age, especially with concurrent heart and kidney problems. Aspirin, in particular, can cause bleeding. This is the danger if you are on "blood thinning" agents to prevent blood clotting; such as warfarin and low-dose aspirin, among others. Ibuprofen can be used and is relatively safe. It is better to start on a low dose, possibly half the normal adult dose, and slowly increase if necessary. Codeine can also be used. Side effects such as drowsiness and constipation may be pronounced; hence, the lowest effective dose is recommended. Triptans have not been shown to be harmful and can be used, even though they are seldom prescribed in the elderly. Ergot alkaloids should only be used with extreme caution, as they tend to cause blood vessel constriction in the skin, and thus cause cold hands and feet, as well as increase the risk of ischemic heart disease and impaired kidney function.

Nausea and Vomiting:

Phosphorylated sugars are harmless and seem to be effective in treating nausea and vomiting. They do not interact with other medicines. However, great caution must be exercised in diabetic patients, as this is a type of sugar, and can therefore affect the diabetic's blood sugar levels. Cyclizine and buclizine are very effective. As they are not used on a permanent basis, the likelihood of them causing age-related adverse effects is reduced. The sufferer may at most experience sedation, dry mouth, and urine retention with longer periods of treatment. A safe alternative, even when taking other medicines, may be the homeopathic drops, nux vomica. They can be administered directly under the tongue or in a bit of water up to every fifteen minutes in severe cases. They are highly unlikely to cause any adverse reactions to the elderly patient, but check with a homeopath to be certain.

Herbal and Natural Remedies:

St. John's wort should be avoided. It interacts with numerous medicines, and can cause side effects which may be more severe with advancing age. Feverfew is not viewed as safe, as it can affect blood clotting. Magnesium is an excellent choice and should be taken in combination with calcium, so as not to affect the delicate balance between these two elements in the body. In addition, it can alleviate night cramps and give more energy. Vitamin B in recommended doses is safe to use and can help fight fatigue. There may only be one potential problem—with large doses of vitamin B6, the action of L-Dopa in Parkinsonism may be affected. Omega-3 is a safe supplement to take and can enhance general health, reduce risks of heart attacks and strokes, and lower blood cholesterol levels. It may even assist in overall well-being and quality of life in certain illnesses, e.g. Alzheimer's and Parkinson's disease, cancer, and arthritis.

Alternative Treatments:

All of the alternative treatments mentioned in this book are suitable in the elderly. Caution should be exercised with homeopathy, and a registered homeopath should be consulted before self-medicating with any remedies to ensure that there will be no interactions with concurrent conditions and medicines. Belladonna may cause problems and should best be avoided, unless it is prescribed by a homeopath.

Other:

Dietary trigger factors should be eliminated to prevent migraines. Refer to the list of dietary as well as other migraine trigger factors to avoid as many of them as possible, and thereby reduce migraine frequency. Get plenty of rest during an attack, and eliminate noises and offensive smells.

2. PRECAUTIONS

With age, the body tends to slow down a bit and certain organs, enzymes, and systems in the body no longer work as efficiently as they used to. Medicines are usually broken down in the liver and excreted via the kidneys. These vital organs often function less well with increasing age. In addition, many elderly people suffer from other illnesses and take medicines. Therefore, it is very important to note that should you be elderly, taking medicines for certain conditions, and have an illness, then you should be very careful with other remedies and treatments. Always check with your doctor or pharmacist before self-medicating. Medicines tend to interact with each other and certain medical conditions, and this can give rise to unwanted and potentially harmful adverse effects. In addition, dosage adjustments often need to be made to reduce the risk of having side effects. Always tell your health care professional about the medicines you are taking, as well as any medical conditions you may be suffering from.

The good news is that migraines occur less frequently with advancing age. Should you have a sudden onset of severe, blinding pain at your temples, when you have not suffered from a migraine in a long time, then you should see your doctor immediately.

For an easy overview, the following table has been included.

The key: *Safe* = Yes, can safely be used by all groups.

Avoid = Should be avoided because of known adverse effects, or because there is insufficient information regarding its safe use in a particular condition.

Caution = Can be used with caution, in certain conditions, and **only** with the prior approval of a registered health care practitioner.

Please note that should you be considering any of these treatment options and you have any pre-existing medical conditions or are taking any other medicines, then you should first check with your doctor, pharmacist, or alternative health care provider beforehand.

	Children	Pregnancy	Lactation	Elderly
PAIN:				
Acetaminophen	Safe	Safe	Safe	Safe
Aspirin	Avoid	Avoid	Avoid	Caution
Ibuprofen	Safe	Avoid	Caution	Caution
Mefenamic acid	Safe	Avoid	Avoid	Caution
Codeine	Caution	Avoid	Caution	Safe
Triptans	Avoid	Caution	Caution	Caution
Ergot alkaloids	Avoid	Avoid	Avoid	Caution
NAUSEA/ VOMITING:				
Phosphorylated sugars	Safe	Safe	Safe	Safe
Cyclizine	Caution	Avoid	Caution	Caution
Buclizine	Avoid	Safe	Caution	Safe
Nux vomica	Safe	Safe	Safe	Caution
HERBAL:				
Feverfew	Avoid	Avoid	Avoid	Caution
St. John's wort	Avoid	Avoid	Avoid	Caution
Kava kava	Avoid	Avoid	Avoid	Caution
SUPPLEMENTS:				
Magnesium	Safe	Safe	Safe	Safe
Vitamin B	Safe	Safe	Caution	Safe
Omega-3	Safe	Safe	Safe	Safe
TMG	Caution	Caution	Caution	Safe
ALTERNATIVE:				
Homeopathy	Safe	Caution	Caution	Caution
Tissue Salts	Safe	Safe	Safe	Safe
Aromatherapy	Safe	Caution	Safe	Safe
Reflexology	Safe	Caution	Safe	Safe
Acupuncture	Safe	Caution	Safe	Safe
Massage	Safe	Safe	Safe	Safe
Chiropractic	Safe	Caution	Safe	Safe
Yoga	Safe	Caution	Safe	Safe
PMA	Caution	Safe	Safe	Safe
Diet	Safe	Safe	Safe	Safe

Table showing which treatments can be used in certain special cases of migraine sufferers.

CHAPTER 12

Lifestyle Modifications

Possibly the most unwanted advice to any patient is to make lifestyle changes. It seems so difficult to change a known routine, but if the pain is bad enough, these changes can make a significant difference. It may be challenging to begin with, but in the end, once results are noticeable, it will have been worth it.

- Avoiding foods, drinks, and other trigger factors that cause migraines will reduce the frequency and severity of your migraines. Identifying your own specific trigger factors is the most difficult part. Refer back to the list of common dietary trigger factors, and try to remove them from your life. Re-introduce them back slowly, one by one. Soon you will be able to identify which substances may be problematic for you. Avoid them in future, to the best of your ability.

- Try to eat regular meals, and try not to skip them. The healthiest diet is a diabetic one, with five to six smaller meals spaced throughout the day, as opposed to eating only one or two big meals. By eating regularly, you can avoid a sudden drop in blood sugar levels, and can thereby prevent a migraine. Maintaining constant blood sugar levels can make a significant difference to migraine prevention. Try to avoid too many refined sugars, such as in sweets, biscuits, chocolates, and certain cool drinks, which cause a rapid peak in blood sugar levels, but also a fast drop thereafter. Start to eat more complex carbohydrates, such as in fruit, muesli, and vegetables, which are released more gradually into the blood, thereby preventing the sudden rise and drop in blood sugar levels.

- Drink up to eight glasses of water per day to flush out any toxins. A build-up of metabolic or dietary wastes can cause a migraine.

- Treat factors causing stress, if you can. Stress causes migraines, which in turn aggravates your stress, and the situation gets progressively worse. Making a life-changing decision may be necessary to eliminate harmful stress.

- Find more time to relax and to do hobbies that make you happy. In addition, sleep regular hours. Avoid sleeping in too long on weekends when you have had sleep deprivation during the week. Sleep is healing, but too much sleep can be almost as detrimental to your health as too little. Most people need between six and nine hours of sleep per night. This varies from person to person, but try to identify how much sleep you need in order to function optimally during the day.

- Stop smoking if you are a smoker. Smoking affects your blood vessels and lungs and can cause migraines. In addition, you may feel far more energetic once you have stopped smoking, which in turn will reduce stress levels. Try to stay away from heavy smokers, as passive smoking, by constantly inhaling cigarette smoke, can also trigger a migraine.

- Regular exercise can help to prevent migraines. Heavy contact or high-impact sports are not recommended, as these can bring on a migraine. Yoga, Callanetics, tai chi, swimming, Pilates, and other stretching exercises may help to relax and thereby prevent migraines. Avoid exercise, however, while you are suffering from a migraine, because this can make it a lot worse. During an attack, it is best to lie down in a dark, quiet room and relax.

- Avoid overly hot baths or saunas, as these can cause vasodilation, resulting in a migraine. This probably will affect you more while you are suffering from a migraine.

- Every now and again, it may not be a bad idea to detoxify

your system. Many alternative therapists believe that if the toxins in your system are eliminated, then migraines will be sorted out. A popular belief is that if the liver is toxic, then migraines will occur. The liver is a very important organ of the body. Its main function is to detoxify chemicals in the body via numerous enzyme systems. If the liver is sick, e.g. hepatitis, jaundice, or cirrhosis, or overloaded, e.g. dietary excesses such as alcohol and fats, then it no longer functions as effectively as it should. Most medicines, including painkillers, are detoxified in the liver, and taking too may of them can also stress the liver. A backlog is then created, and the body produces symptoms of toxicity, which include migraines.

There are many detoxification programs available, all of which include drinking up to two liters of water per day. Have a day of only eating or drinking water, fruit juices, fruit, vegetables, and clear soups. In addition, it is also a good idea to stop the intake of alcohol, caffeine, and fats during a day of detoxification. Liver protectors such milk thistle may help in the future to keep your liver healthy. There are numerous commercially available detox programs. Ask your pharmacist, homeopath, dietician, or alternative healthcare practitioner for a recommendation.

Be cautious, however, when doing a detox program. The sudden withdrawal of caffeine or not eating at all may precipitate a migraine attack in sensitive people. Rather, in this case, gradually reduce the intake of caffeine or merely remove "unnatural" foods from your diet, such as foods containing preservatives, artificial sweeteners, colorants, or flavorings. Remember, that the more wholesome your diet the less likely it is to cause migraines. Although it may often be a simpler option to indulge in convenience foods or fast foods, this is definitely not the best choice if you suffer from migraines. All these convenience or fast foods contain plenty of preservatives, colorants, and artificial flavors among other things, all of which can precipitate a migraine.

Some trigger factors are unavoidable, such as weather, hormones, and noises. However, by avoiding those you can control, you may find that the other factors affect you less. Being exposed to more than one trigger factor at a time can have a greater potential to cause a migraine, whereas a minimal exposure to a single trigger factor on its own may not even affect you at all.

CHAPTER 13

Migraine Diary

Start up a headache chart, in which you note down particulars concerning your migraines. Keep this journal active for at least a month, but preferably longer, especially if you are on prophylactic (preventative) therapy. This enables you to monitor your migraine frequency and severity and to identify trigger factors. The longer you keep this chart going, the more accurately you will be able to see patterns developing, e.g. if you are a woman, you may notice that migraines occur around the time of your menstrual period. It will also help you to determine which remedies aid in alleviating your pain, from painkillers, to vitamins, to alternative therapies. Furthermore, it can help your doctor treat you more effectively and monitor your progress.

Date:

Time of Onset: When did the migraine begin?

Location of pain: Shade in the painful areas on diagrams such as these.

Type of pain: Describe whether the pain was constant and dull, throbbing, sharp, piercing, or viselike.

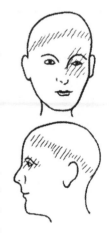

Signs and Symptoms: Include if there is an aura or a prodrome, where theyare present, as well as all other signs and symptoms experienced during a migraine.

Trigger factors: Think of possible trigger factors that you have been exposed to prior to the onset of the migraine. Refer to the box on common trigger factors mentioned previously to help you jog your memory.

Severity: Rate the severity of the migraine from 1 to 5, with 1 being mild and manageable, and 5 being so severe and debilitating that you are unable to function.

1   2   3   4   5

Treatments used: Note what medicines or treatments you have used, whether they have worked, and when pain relief became effective. Include natural and alternative remedies. Mention the number and frequency of doses required before relief was achieved, in the case of medicines.

Notes: Jot down any other information that may be relevant, e.g. stage of menstrual cycle, starting a new medical treatment for another complaint, illness, taking a different herbal remedy, or trying out a different alternative therapy. Any change in lifestyle and stress levels may be relevant.

CHAPTER 14

Long-term Expectations

A migraine may last from a few hours up to three days. Childhood migraines may disappear at puberty, and likewise, migraines may start at puberty and go through to adulthood. Generally migraine sufferers will have had migraines before the age of thirty years, and these may continue throughout their lives, but become less severe and less frequent as they age. Often migraines will disappear completely after the age of forty-five years.

If prophylactic treatment is applied for at least six months, migraine frequency and severity improve markedly. Treatment regimens must be followed precisely in order for them to work effectively. Often, various different therapies need to be tried out before an effective one is found, because not all treatments are effective on all people. It is important not to give up too soon, and also not to keep changing doctors if a particular therapy does not work. Rather inform your doctor, and then he or she can guide you into a different dosage regimen or new treatment. Remember that it takes some time for certain therapies to take effect. You may not see results immediately.

If migraines are infrequent, then it is best to treat them when they occur by using suitable painkillers, such as mentioned in the chapter "Treatment of Migraines." You could try some alternative or complimentary therapies, such as reflexology or acupuncture, to alleviate migraines. Lifestyle adjustments will go a long way to improving your quality of life, because trigger factors are being avoided. Keep a headache diary and identify problem areas. You will benefit from monitoring potential trigger factors and avoiding them.

Migraines can severely impact a sufferer's life. Therefore it is a good idea to follow some of the guidelines mentioned above, make a few lifestyle changes, and thereby improve your general quality of life. There are still more migraine-free days than days of suffering with migraines, and that thought makes it all a lot more bearable.

There are many famous people who were known to suffer from migraines, but that did not deter them from achieving what they did. Examples are Julius Caesar, Lewis Carroll (thought to have been inspired to write *Alice in Wonderland* during migraine hallucinations), Vincent van Gogh, Napoleon Bonaparte, Elvis Presley, Virginia Woolf, Charles Darwin, Joan of Arc, Sigmund Freud, Peter Tchaikovsky, and Pablo Picasso, among others. It is still possible to live a fulfilling, successful life with migraines, as all these people have demonstrated through their achievements.

With all the research that has gone into migraine treatments and prevention, you too will find something to help reduce the severity and frequency of your migraines. Be willing to try, and you should succeed.

Glossary

Analgesic   A medicine used to relieve pain.

Agonist   A substance which has the ability to enhance or potentiate an action or response.

Antagonist   A substance which has the ability to prevent or counteract an action or response.

Anaphylactic Shock A rare, life-threatening allergic response in a hypersensitive individual to a substance, causing the airway to close; the face, body, and tongue to swell; itchy hives and/or patches to appear all over the body; and heart failure. The response is due to the release of a mediator in the body, called histamine. Treatment must be immediate, because the reaction proceeds from mild to life-threatening very quickly.

Anti-emetic   A medicine used to treat vomiting. Often also useful in treating nausea.

Anti-inflammatory A medicine used to treat inflammation in the body, which presents with pain, redness, heat, swelling, and loss of normal movement or function.

Beta-Blocker   A medicine which blocks certain adrenaline sites in the body, which are called beta-receptors, thereby preventing a reaction via that receptor when adrenaline tries to bind to it.

Calcium Channel Blocker   A medicine which blocks an exchange mechanism for calcium in the body. This medicine is usually used to treat heart or blood pressure disorders.

Cardiovascular	Anything relating to the heart and blood vessels, which transport blood around the body.
Diuretic	A medicine which is known as a "water pill" because of its ability to remove excess water from the body via the kidney and bladder.
Enzymes	Protein-like substances which control metabolic processes in the body that are vital to the normal functions of a living organism. They catalyze/bring about certain reactions.
GABA	The abbreviation for gamma amino butyric acid, which is a neurotransmitter substance in the brain, causing relaxation.
Inflammation	A response by the body to injury. Symptoms and signs of inflammation include pain, redness, heat, swelling, and loss of normal movement or function.
Inorganic	A substance that is not derived from a living organism. These substances include minerals and salts.
Interaction	The reaction between substances, medicinal, herbal, or chemicals existing naturally within the body, which can result in harmful effects.
MAOI	The abbreviation for monoamine oxidase inhibitors, which are medicines that block the breakdown of monoamine substances in the body, such as serotonin, adrenaline, and dopamine.
Mediator	A substance in the body which carries information and can bring about various chain reactions.

Musculoskeletal	The relationship between muscles and bones in the body.
Neurotransmitter	A chemical released by the nerves, which aids in the transmission of information in the brain and body. Examples include serotonin, noradrenaline, dopamine, and acetylcholine.
Pallor	Loss of color in the skin, causing it to become pale.
Pilules	Tiny, round sugar balls, which are used for administering homeopathic medicines.
Placebo	An inactive dosage form, e.g. tablet or capsule, which looks identical to the active dosage form, except that it lacks the active substance.
Prophylactic	A medicine which is used as a preventative measure.
Receptor	A site in the body to which certain hormones, chemicals, and other substances attach, thereby bringing about an effect.
Serotonin	A hormonal substance in the body which has numerous actions, including neurotransmitter functions, mood, sleep, blood clotting, pain, and appetite control.
Sinuses	Cavities in the skull, around the eyes, and in the cheekbones and forehead.
SSRI	The abbreviation for selective serotonin re-uptake inhibitor. This is a medicine which increases the amount of serotonin available between nerve cells by preventing it from being reabsorbed up by the nerves.

Syndrome	A collection of specific signs and symptoms, which together cause a condition.
Tincture	An alcoholic mixture containing a medicine.
Tolerance	This occurs when the body gets used to a chemical substance being in the body, and then no longer produces the desired effect unless the dosage is increased. This is often the result of overuse or abuse of a substance.
Tranquilizer	A medicine which relaxes and sedates a person.
Tricyclic Antidepressant	A medicine which treats depression. Its chemical structure contains three rings which are attached to each other. This medicine binds to certain receptors and thereby exerts its antidepressant effect.
Vascular	Anything relating to the blood vessels.
Vasoconstriction	The narrowing of blood vessels.
Vasodilation	The widening of blood vessels.

References

British National Formulary, 46th Edition. September 2003, *http:// bnf.org/bnf.*

Clough, C. "Treating migraine." *British Medical Journal,* 1989.

Daily Drug Use, Revised Edition. The Pharmaceutical Society of South Africa, 2001.

Digby, Berkley. "Classical Homeopathic Remedies for Common Ailments." *Pharma Natura,* 1996.

Fabian, June and Lee Baker. "What a Headache Those XX Chromosomes Can Be!" *The Journal of Modern Pharmacy,* July 2001.

Holford, Patrick and James Braly. *The H-Factor Solution.* North Bergen, N.J.: Basic Health Publications, Inc., 2003.

Katzung, Bertram G. *Basic and Clinical Pharmacology, 6th Edition.* Appleton and Lange, 1995.

Martindale. *The Extra Pharmacopoeia, 13th Edition.* London: The Pharmaceutical Press, 1993.

Medical Dictionary, Brockhampton Reference. London: Brockhampton Press, 1995.

The Merck Manual, 16th Edition. Rahway, N.J.: Merck & Co., Inc., 1992.

Mindell, Earl. *The Vitamin Bible.* Horsham: Biblios Ltd., 1995.

Peatfield, R. "How to treat migraine." *British Journal of Hospital Medicine,* 1984.

"Migraine: Current concepts in pathogenesis and treatment." *Drugs,* 1983.

Schlebusch, Lourens. *Mind Shift, Stress Management and Your Health.* Durban: University of Natal Press, 2000.

South African Medicines Formulary, 4th Edition. Cape Town: Department of Pharmacology, University of Cape Town, 1997.

Theron, F. and C.J.F. Grobler. "Contraception, Theory and Practice." *Academica,* Pretoria, 1992.

Urbaniak, E. *Natural Healing for Headaches.* Washington: Harbor Press, 2000.

USP DI- Volume I, Advice for the Health Care Professional, 18th Edition. Rockville, Maryland, 1998.

USP DI - Volume II, Advice for the Patient, 18th Edition. Rockville, Maryland, 1998.

van der Merwe, Arien. *All About Cold Water Salmon Oil.* South Africa: Formule Naturelle Publishing.

White, A. *A Guide to Biochemistry, The Homeopathic Chemist.* Cape Town: Plein Street.

Index

About the Author

Claire Houlding (*nee* Claassens) was born in South Africa. She started suffering from migraine headaches from about 6 years of age. The migraines have continued throughout her life and therefore inspired her to not only research, but also try, their countless treatment alternatives. She studied pharmacy at Rhodes University, graduating with distinction. Claire has worked as a retail pharmacist since graduation and managed, in her professional capacity, to help many desperate sufferers deal with their debilitating pain.

Having been in a state of desperation herself, by suffering with blinding migraines, she was able to assist patients from a professional as well as personal perspective. In addition, she has arranged private consultations, given talks and appeared on radio. Her success in empowering innumerable patients to deal effectively with their pain, inspired her to write *Managing Migraines*, so that she could reach many more sufferers and provide them with the many treatment alternatives accessible to them. It has been very important to Claire to explore all effective treatment alternatives available in the management of migraines, not only from a pharmaceutical standpoint, but also from an alternative, complementary and dietary perspective. She decided to include all these various options, as well as useful lifestyle modifications in her book, in order to broaden the horizons of the many inadequately treated sufferers worldwide.

She has successfully managed to reduce the frequency and severity of her own migraines so significantly, that she wrote *Managing Migraines* to share her knowledge and experience with other sufferers, so that they too may gain relief from their physical anguish.

Claire currently resides in Vancouver, WA with her husband and son.

Printed in the United Kingdom
by Lightning Source UK Ltd.
132940UK00002B/174/A